LEGENDARY HUNTERS
OF THE
SOUTHERN HIGHLANDS

LEGENDARY HUNTERS
OF THE
SOUTHERN
HIGHLANDS

A Century of Sport and Survival
in the Great Smoky Mountains

BOB PLOTT

THE
History
PRESS

Published by The History Press
Charleston, SC 29403
www.historypress.net

Copyright © 2009 by Bob Plott
All rights reserved

First published 2009

Manufactured in the United States

ISBN 978.1.59629.703.6

Library of Congress Cataloging-in-Publication Data
Plott, Bob.
Legendary hunters of the southern highlands : a century of sport and survival in the Great Smoky Mountains / Bob Plott.
p. cm.
Includes bibliographical references.
ISBN 978-1-59629-703-6
1. Hunters--Great Smoky Mountains (N.C. and Tenn.)--Biography. 2. Mountaineers--Great Smoky Mountains (N.C. and Tenn.)--Biography. 3. Great Smoky Mountains (N.C. and Tenn.)--Biography. 4. Plott, Bob--Family. 5. Hunting--Great Smoky Mountains (N.C. and Tenn.)--History. 6. Mountain life--Great Smoky Mountains (N.C. and Tenn.)--History. 7. Outdoor life--Great Smoky Mountains (N.C. and Tenn.)--History. 8. Wilderness survival--Great Smoky Mountains (N.C. and Tenn.)--History. 9. Great Smoky Mountains (N.C. and Tenn.)--Social life and customs. I. Title.
SK113.P55 2009
799.292'273--dc22
[B]
2009040104

Notice: The information in this book is true and complete to the best of our knowledge. It is offered without guarantee on the part of the author or The History Press. The author and The History Press disclaim all liability in connection with the use of this book.

All rights reserved. No part of this book may be reproduced or transmitted in any form whatsoever without prior written permission from the publisher except in the case of brief quotations embodied in critical articles and reviews.

*This book is dedicated to the memory of Robert Henry Plott,
Tom Alexander and "Little" George Plott—men who truly matched our
magnificent Great Smoky Mountains.*

CONTENTS

Acknowledgements	9
Introduction	11
The Other Plott Boys	13
Many Privations to Endure	23
Man on a Mission	31
The Next Generations	41
Little George	73
Citizen Soldier	87
Christmas Eve 1944	95
"A Woods Roving Family"	103
The Fie Top Bear War	123
Not Nary a One	135
Duyuktv—The Right Way	151
Bibliography	157
About the Author	159

ACKNOWLEDGEMENTS

For me, the most enjoyable part of writing books is the research that goes into it. More significantly, it is the friends you make in the process. It was no different with this project. And, in fact, it was even more rewarding in that I was able to reconnect with family members and in some cases help mend some bridges among feuding factions.

As always, there are far too many people who have helped me to list them all. However, a few deserve special mention: George Ellison helped me get started writing and has played an integral role as my editor, advisor and, most importantly, my friend. The same can be said for Lynn and Ann Moretz, who have proven to be my tireless supporters, both personally and professionally.

I am honored to be related to Ernestine Upchurch, whom I refer to as the "Godmother of the Maggie Valley Mountain Mafia." She is always there when we need her and she always finds a way to get things done. Through her I have met many other wonderful folks like Tony, Steven and Linda Rich, Judy Alexander Coker and Charlie Clement, as well as relatives David and Shane Plott, Louise Plott, Marty Plott Moody, Nancy Moody, Crystal Ramm and Bart Campbell.

Learning from the eighty-eight-year-old dynamo Louise Plott, wife of the late Herbert Plott Jr., was indeed a privilege and a pleasure. And Steve and Linda Rich are now valued close friends, as is Judy Alexander Coker. Judy, her sister Alice and their families continue the legacy of their parents, Tom and Judy Alexander, in running the finest resort in the Great Smoky Mountains—Cataloochee Ranch.

Acknowledgements

Meeting Wayne Battle at a book signing was an incredible blessing. Not only is he a relative but he is also a dear friend and mentor. Through him I met two more amazing ladies, Helen Luckadoo and Carmen Plott, who both proved to be delightfully insightful. James and Ann Plott also provided interesting perspective and stories.

Getting a state historical marker approved honoring the Plott hound was gratifying on many levels, but none more so than reconnecting with Ruth Plott and her son Bill. Both have proven to be valuable sources of information. Bill has the eagle eye of the world's best editors and helps keep me accurate and honest. Ruth has turned into a world-class researcher and has been extremely helpful to me.

So too have Elizabeth Plott, Jay Plott and Fonda Martin. Cousin Lizzie has carried on the rich tradition of her father and grandfather as a family historian. Talking with her always brightens my day. Thanks also to Johnny Plott, Bebe Abel and Madeline Plott Dammonn.

I wish Dewey Sharp could have lived to see this book published. But I thank my friends Marshall McClung and Tommy Wilcox for introducing me to him. And special thanks to Ann Moore of the Foxfire Foundation and Annette Hartigan, librarian of the Great Smoky Mountains National Park.

Some old friends also deserve mention. John Jackson has repeatedly proven to be a true friend, mentor, spiritual advisor and hunting partner to me. Charles Brown, woodsman extraordinaire, has stuck with me through thick and thin and I look forward to many future adventures with him. Earl Lanning has been like a second father to me. I will never forget his generosity and guidance, nor the sweet kindness of his late beloved wife, Bonnie. Thanks also to Mike Pritchard, Tom Deloach, Daniel Whitener, Mark Baker, Steve Fielder, Mike Alton, Billy Chapman, Harry Noel, John Young, Roy Carter, William Carter, Matt Mull, Rick Davis, Jeff Crisp, Frank Methven, Ben Lilly and Rex Patterson. Special thanks to David Brewin and Scott Philyaw of Western Carolina University.

Last, but certainly not least, I thank my immediate family—my wife Janice, my son Jacob and my mother Mary. Thanks also to my niece Katy Talbert for her computer and photography expertise. You all are the best! Thank you for putting up with me and for your undying support.

INTRODUCTION

My objectives in writing my first book, *Strike and Stay—The Story of the Plott Hound*, were simple: I wanted to pay homage to my family and our magnificent dogs. And I wanted my son to have an accurate record of this history to share one day with his own children and grandchildren.

In researching that first book, I found an abundance of fascinating regional historical information. Yet much of it had to be edited out because it did not fit the format of the story. Nevertheless, it was intriguing and I felt that it needed to be shared, which led me to write my second book, *A History of Hunting in the Great Smoky Mountains*.

However, much excellent material had to be edited out or omitted from this book too. But yet again, I felt that it needed to be shared. The question was, how? Should a third book have some sort of unifying theme pertaining to hunting in the Great Smoky Mountains? Or should it stand alone as a separate collection of mountain hunting stories without a connecting thread or theme?

Free-standing individual stories could definitely work. After all, one of my writing idols—John Parris—wrote several outstanding books about colorful, random characters and places in southern mountain folklore. And my friend and mentor George Ellison had used a similar format with great success in his fine book, *Mountain Passages*. I could certainly do a lot worse than attempting to emulate either of these master wordsmiths.

But as I reviewed my research, three underlying themes continued to prevail. Aside from being master woodsmen, all of these mountaineers had

Introduction

three things in common: First, their families had all hunted for a century or more in the Great Smoky Mountains. Second, almost all of them had some connection to one another—in most cases they were related, while others were simply friends or neighbors. And finally, all of them in some way had made significant but mostly little-known contributions to southern mountain culture. Some of their contributions were truly heroic. Yet others provide us with a legacy of a simple bygone era of totally self-sufficient mountain living. It is a study of a lifestyle that few, if any, people practice today. These folks knew what it was actually like to work in logging camps, make moonshine, hunt for survival, farm for a living and fight for what they believed in. They actually lived it. Theirs is a story of classic but obscure Americana.

Thus, the title and theme of my third book had finally come together—*Legendary Hunters of the Southern Highlands: A Century of Sport and Survival in the Great Smoky Mountains.*

I should mention that much of the background information regarding these characters is not always specifically related to the sport of hunting. However, I included it because I felt strongly that it was important in how it shaped and impacted their hunting and personal lives and, just as importantly, in how it impacted southern mountain culture and how we are often perceived by others. I found the character of these mountaineers to be intriguing, and I believe that you will as well.

As usual, I have included a good deal of scholarly historical documentation in this project. But a fair amount of the book is devoted to first- or secondhand accounts of living family members or friends. In some cases it is an oral history of *real* stories, by the *real* people who actually experienced them.

Lately it seems that we often forget the enjoyment behind hearing and telling a good story. It's much easier to watch a video or surf the Internet. But if we care anything about our future, we should preserve and protect our oral histories before they are lost forever. Just as importantly, we should learn from them.

I hope that I did these stories justice. If so, perhaps one hundred years from now future generations of mountaineers will be gathered around a campfire remembering these hunting legends that came before them.

THE OTHER PLOTT BOYS

Dating back to the times of the early Cherokee warriors, Haywood County, North Carolina, has been a haven for some of the most celebrated hunters in Smoky Mountain history. Stories still abound today of old-time hunting legends like the great Cherokee chiefs Yonaguska and Junaluska, as well as Israel "Wid" Medford, Fredrick "Uncle Fed" Messer and "Turkey" George Palmer, just to name a few.

However, few Haywood County hunting clans can match the notoriety of the Plott family. Many of the Plotts were hunters without peer, but it is their world-renowned hunting dogs—the Plott bear hound—that they are best known for.

Family patriarch George (Johannes) Plott is generally thought to have brought the breed to America in 1750. However, recent research indicates that it may have actually been as early as 1741. It is possible that his name was never Johannes, but always George—and contrary to popular belief, it certainly was *never* Jonathan.

Nevertheless, it is an indisputable fact that by 1800 Henry Plott—one of George's three sons—had taken part of the family pack to settle and hunt on what is now Plott Creek in western Haywood County. The Plott family flourished here, eventually acquiring almost two thousand acres of the beautiful watershed that became known as Plott Valley, surrounded by the towering mountain range now called the Plott Balsams.

By 1820, Henry and his wife Lydia had eleven children, eight of them boys—Osborne, Jonathan, Henry Jr., Enos, John T., Amos, George and David. As the Plott lads grew into adulthood, they all, to some degree,

"Turkey" George Palmer. *Cataloochee Ranch Collection.*

developed and refined their clan's superb farming, hunting and animal husbandry skills. George and Osborne Plott eventually relocated to Georgia and Alabama, respectively, while Jonathan migrated to the eastern part of Haywood County, where he built a huge farm in the Pigeon River Valley complete with a sawmill, gristmill and wheelwright shop. Henry Jr. chose to raise his family in Clay County, North Carolina, and two of his brothers, David and Amos, elected to make their homes near what is now known as Maggie Valley, North Carolina. Enos Plott

The Other Plott Boys

Above: Jonathan Plott Mill on Pigeon River. *Plott Family Collection.*

Below: Montraville Plott and sheep dog, circa 1890. *Plott Family Collection.*

settled about halfway between Plott and Maggie Valleys. John T. Plott was the only son who decided to stay at the site of the original family home—Plott Valley. And it was John T. Plott and his descendants who have been credited with most of the success pertaining to the perpetuation of the family hunting dogs.

John T. Plott, son of Henry Plott, father of Montraville Plott. *Plott Family Collection.*

Much has been written—and rightfully so—about the roles that John T. Plott, his son Montraville "Mont" Plott and his grandsons (John A., Vaughn, George and Samuel) played in the development of the Plott family dogs.

The Other Plott Boys

These Plott men were all instrumental in the Plott hound becoming one of the most coveted breeds of big game hunting dogs that the world has ever known. Most of them were world-class hunters as well.

But the "other" Plott boys—particularly the Maggie Valley–area Plott brothers and their descendants, along with their Plott Creek cousin, George Ellis Plott—were outstanding hunters and dog breeders in their own right. Very little has been written about them, but their story is no less remarkable than that of their other family members. It just is not as well known. This is their story.

AMOS, ENOS AND DAVID PLOTT

The exact date that the Plott brothers moved to the Maggie Valley area—known as Jonathan Creek and Ivy Hill until 1926—is unknown. Historian W.C. Allen described Jonathan Creek as "a meandering mountain torrent, rising among the peaks and winding through a beautiful valley with lofty mountains on either side as it widens into the Pigeon River." The creek was named for Jonathan McPeters, a Revolutionary War veteran who had claimed land there in 1787.

David Plott settled on the upper waters of Jonathan Creek, near the present location of Maggie Valley School, about 1825. Amos Plott moved

Amos Plott Cabin, Maggie Valley, North Carolina. *Plott Family Collection*.

to the area about 1832. He lived on the other side of the stream on a ridge above Campbell Creek. His cabin, built in the 1830s, is still standing on Johnson Branch Road. Enos Plott was soon to follow. His home was high above Jonathan Creek, near the community of Saunook, at an elevation of over three thousand feet.

While their exact relocation dates are unclear, their reasons for moving to the Jonathan Creek area are obvious: the huge, lush valley surrounded by mountains was virtually unsettled and provided the same farming and hunting opportunities for the Plott brothers that Plott Valley had provided for their father Henry. In short, it was a near perfect place to farm, bear hunt and raise cattle, horses, sheep and hunting dogs.

The location that the Plott boys chose to settle also tells us a lot about their primary concerns and interests. Though David Plott was indeed an avid hunter and houndsman—probably as good as his brothers—he nevertheless made his living farming in the valley. Amos and Enos, on the other hand, were passionate woodsmen and hunters. Each were often employed as guides, and both (especially Amos) were widely recognized as the best hunters in the region. Smaller log cabins, deep in the woods and closer to game trails, were more ideally suited for these dedicated "ridge runners." Amos and Enos Plott plunged headlong into a life devoted entirely to bear hunting behind their beloved Plott dogs.

While Amos Plott's home survives today and one of his hunting rifles remains a treasured family heirloom, we unfortunately have no pictures and only a few documented stories about this iconic frontiersman. In *Strike and Stay—The Story of the Plott Hound*, I described the exploits of Amos Plott:

> *Amos, like quite a few of the Plotts, myself included, was left-handed. This trait served him well, probably saving his life on another early bear hunt. The Plott legacy contends that Amos's dogs had struck a bear trail, and while being hotly pursued the wounded bruin sought refuge from them in a large hole where a tree had been uprooted.*
>
> *Closely behind, Amos soon arrived to find his hounds holding the bear at bay in the hole. The bear was firmly entrenched there at an awkward angle and the dogs were unable to reach him. Amos surveyed the situation, and unable to get off a shot with his muzzleloading rifle, he decided his only option was to try and kill the bear with his knife. He then wrapped his right arm to provide it some protection, as he intended to use it as a shield while he attempted with his stronger left hand to kill the bruin with his*

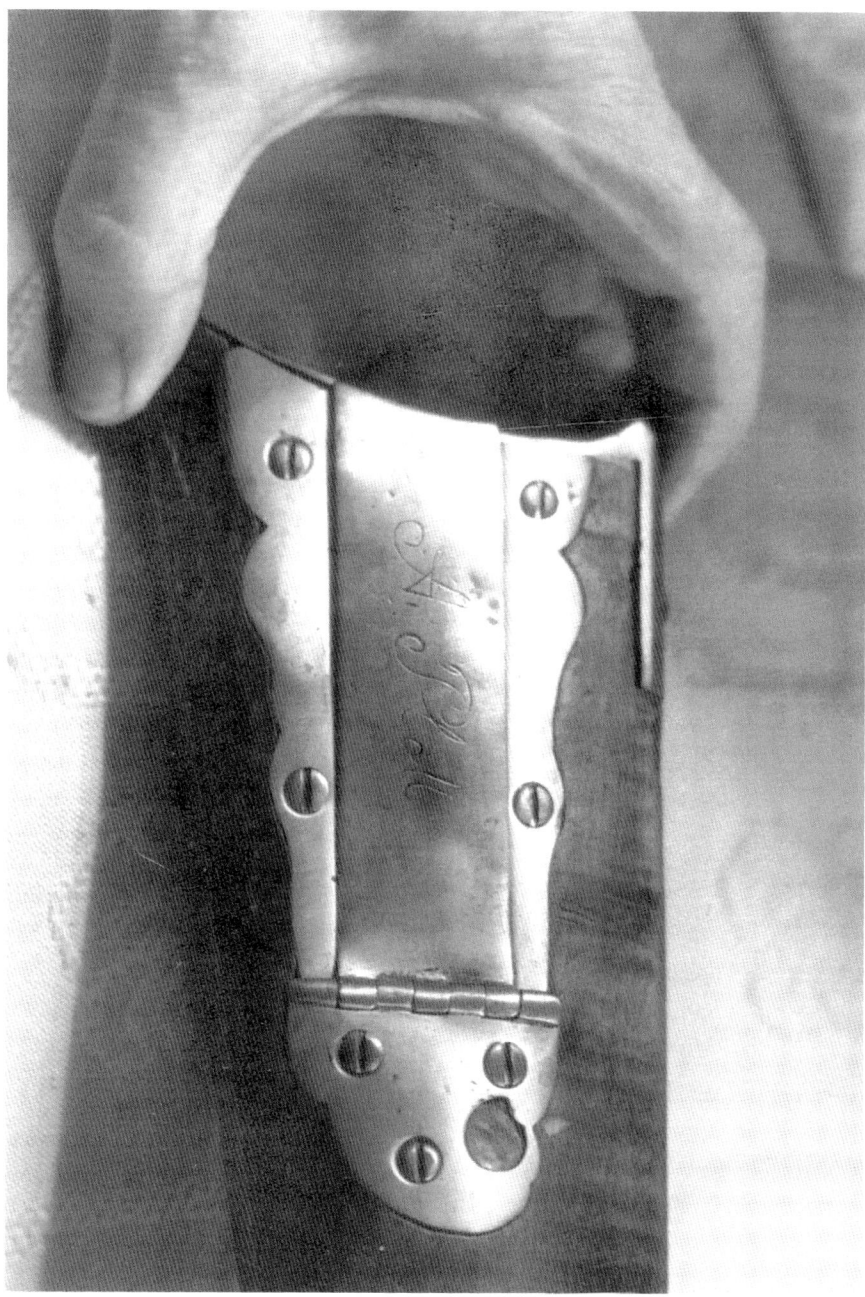

Amos Plott's rifle. Note the name on the patch box. *Courtesy of John Jackson.*

knife. From the only angle available to him, a fierce fight ensued as Amos blocked with his right hand and attacked with his left. He was pretty badly ripped up, but he finally managed to kill the bear. Others in the party said that Amos was drenched in blood from head to toe and nearly bled to death as the hunting party returned home.

Amos fully recovered and continued to hunt and raise dogs until he was an old man. He and his brother Enos also served as guides for Arnold Guyot, the noted Swiss geographer, on some of his trips into the Smokies in 1856, 1857, 1859 and 1860, or at least those in the Balsam Mountain range. Guyot, in appreciation for the help of the Plott men, named two mountains after them, Amos Plott Balsam and Enos Plott Balsam. Amos Plott Balsam, a towering 6,292-foot peak, is now known as Waterrock Knob. However, in an early Guyot map, dated 1864 in the Special Collections area of Hunter Library at Western Carolina University, it is indeed noted as Amos Plott Balsam.

Another peak in the Balsam Range was once known as Brother Plott. Some historians say that it was named in honor of David Plott, while others contend that it was for another Plott brother. No one knows for sure.

Other than the fact that he served as guide to Guyot and was considered to be an equal of his younger brother Amos as a bear hunter, we know little else about the adventures of Enos Plott. However, one amazing story about him is still told by the Plott family today. I first heard it from Hub Plott when I was just a boy. Enos was hunting along the Tennessee border near Walnut Bottom when his hounds struck a bear trail. The race was a hot one as Plott followed his dogs closely. Suddenly, both the hounds and the bear disappeared. They had fallen into a deep but narrow ravine and were trapped there in a fighting frenzy.

Plott quickly considered his options and concluded that he had no other recourse than to try a risky shot into the fracas. He hoped and prayed that he would not hit one of his dogs. But before he could get off a shot, Enos slipped and fell head over heels into the cleft in the midst of the savage bear fight. He had lost his gun, and the angry beast turned its attention from the dogs to maul Plott's left shoulder and arm. Enos figured he was a goner, but he managed to get his folding Barlow knife out of his pocket. He opened it with his teeth as the bear gnawed on him. Plott then stabbed the bear repeatedly as his dogs continued the attack from the flanks and rear. Finally, after what seemed like forever, the bruin died. Badly wounded, Enos managed to climb out of the ravine as his hunting partners arrived to doctor him and carry him back home. He healed quickly, and it wasn't long before he was hunting again.

A common misperception about these early hunters and their dogs is the number of hounds they usually owned. Even relatively affluent hunters seldom kept more than four or five hunting dogs simply because they could not afford to feed any more than that. Most mountain homesteads had no more than two to four hunting dogs. Amos, Enos and David Plott were exceptions to this rule in that they each kept *two* packs of dogs with about five hounds per pack. The Plott brothers hunted so often that they rotated their dogs to keep them fresh and healthy and to ensure their constant availability.

Enos and Amos Plott kept Plott dogs and hunted bear until their deaths in 1874 and 1865, respectively. Today, Bart Campbell, a great-great-grandson of Amos Plott, lives on almost one thousand acres of land in Maggie Valley and continues the Plott tradition of big game hunting in the Great Smoky Mountains. Great-great-granddaughter Ernestine Upchurch, also of Maggie Valley, is a renowned family historian and expert on southern mountain culture.

As Amos and Enos Plott were developing their reputations as some of the premier guides and bear hunters in the Great Smoky Mountains, David Plott, the fifth son of Henry Plott, was making a name for himself as both a farmer and hunter down in the valley along Jonathan Creek. David carried a big bore hunting rifle—a .50-caliber muzzleloader—that had plenty of knock-down power for big game. He put the rifle and his family Plott dogs to good use in harvesting many a bear. That rifle, a percussion cap gun, had probably been converted from an original flintlock that likely dates back to the late eighteenth century. It is probable that this was Henry Plott's rifle and that it had been handed down to his son. If so, the rifle is more than two hundred years old.

Like his more famous brothers, only a few other specific details are known about David Plott. He married Jonathan Creek native Sara Turner in about 1827. Together they raised five children, three of them sons—Leander, Robert Henry and Hebron Plott. By all accounts, David was a dedicated father and husband who instilled a strong love of the land, the family dogs and bear hunting in his three boys. This first generation of young Jonathan Creek hunters is where the story of the "other" Plott boys takes a tragic turn.

MANY PRIVATIONS TO ENDURE

By 1840—the year that Robert Henry Plott was born—the Plott family and their illustrious hounds had been hunting in America for almost one hundred years (maybe more) and had been living in Haywood County for nearly half a century. The Great Smoky Mountains had not changed much during that time and by any standard could still be considered the wild frontier.

David Plott expected his sons to work hard, and he taught them everything he knew about farming, logging and raising livestock and Plott bear dogs. But he also allowed them time to hunt and fish, and he shared with them everything he knew about wilderness survival, firearms and riding horses. Between their father and their Uncles Amos and Enos, the boys had a wealth of expert sporting knowledge at their disposal—and they took full advantage of it. In addition, David expected the lads to be good students and demanded that they do well in school. Apparently the boys did just that.

All three Plott brothers grew into outstanding young men, but none more so than Robert Henry. By 1860, he had grown into a powerfully built adult standing over six and a half feet tall. He was an exceptional marksman, and he used his long legs and extraordinary endurance to run with his Plott dogs as they chased bears across the Balsam Range. Plott family historians remember Robert as a man of good humor but few words, a physical giant who did not tolerate any sort of insult to friend or family. He also possessed an iron-willed sense of honor and loyalty that would serve him well in the difficult years ahead.

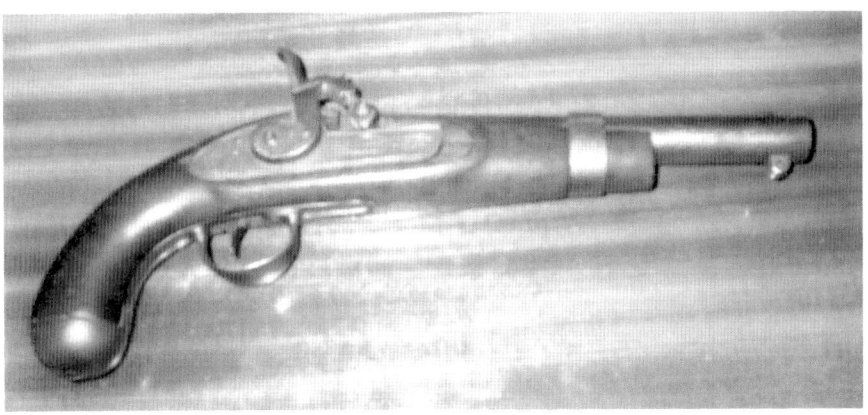

A .54-caliber muzzleloading pistol captured in the Civil War by Robert Henry Plott. *Courtesy of Wayne Battle.*

Robert Plott was planning to attend college at the University of North Carolina, but he put those plans on hold when the Civil War broke out in 1861. He and his brothers stayed home to defend the family farm from renegade bushwhackers and Union troops until 1862, when they joined the Confederate army. Robert, Leander and Hebron Plott were all members of the Sixty-second North Carolina Regiment, a unit made up almost entirely of western North Carolina mountain boys commanded by Colonel Robert Love of nearby Waynesville, North Carolina.

The unit saw quite a bit of action in skirmishes in eastern Tennessee, where they served mostly as guards defending saltworks, railroads and mountain passes. The Plott boys, however, remained unscathed. Robert Henry captured two pistols from enemy combatants during these firefights and either shipped them back to his parents or brought them home while on leave. After the war, Robert would use one of these pistols—a .54-caliber single shot muzzleloader—to hunt bear. The other—a .44-caliber Union officer's side arm—was used for personal protection.

The officers commanding the Sixty-second recognized Robert Plott's sharp shooting skills and issued him a long-range sniper rifle—either a .50-caliber Maynard or a .54-caliber Sharp's. Both of these weapons were breechloading guns well known for their long-range accuracy—well beyond five hundred yards. And both could be loaded from a prone position, making them more advantageous to shooting from hidden locations and harder for the enemy to locate. Unless the Sharp's gun was a captured Union weapon, Plott probably used the Maynard, a rifle much more

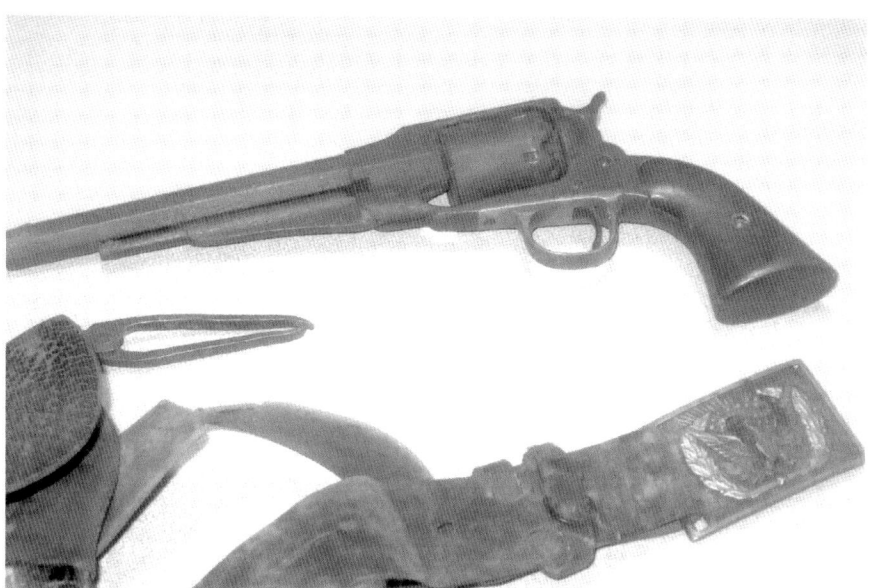

A .44-caliber Union officer's pistol captured in the Civil War by Robert Henry Plott. *Courtesy of Louise Plott.*

common with Confederate troops. It is testament to Robert's sniper skills that in a regiment consisting mostly of sharpshooting mountain hunters, he was one of the few chosen to carry this type of gun. He would later tell his sons of the immense pride he had in the weapon.

In July 1863, their unit was sent to defend the Cumberland Gap under the command of General John Frazier. Frazier had been given very specific orders not to surrender his command. He was to defend the gap at all costs; retreat was acceptable if need be but surrender was *not* an option.

The historic Cumberland Gap—near the borders of Virginia, Tennessee and Kentucky—was of critical importance to the Confederacy, and it was considered to be the strongest naturally defensible position in the south. Union General Ulysses S. Grant said later, in 1864, that "with two brigades of the Army of the Cumberland, I could hold that pass against the army that Napoleon led to Moscow."

General Frazier felt otherwise and, against repeated orders from his superiors, surrendered his men without a shot on September 9, 1863. Of Frazier's men, 600 defied his cowardly order and easily escaped capture. Unfortunately, the Plott brothers were not among that number. They chose instead to obey orders and surrender along with 2,023 of their comrades. Robert Plott was so outraged at Frazier's command that he personally destroyed his treasured Maynard rifle rather than giving it up to the enemy. Though honorable, their surrender would prove to be a tragic mistake for the Plott boys.

Confederate president Jefferson Davis called the surrender "a shameful abandonment of duty." Historians since then have speculated that Frazier was bribed to surrender or that he was simply a Union turncoat. Regardless of the reason, the end result was the same. Robert Henry, Hebron and Leander Plott were headed for Camp Douglas, a Union prisoner of war camp near Chicago, Illinois.

The Plott brothers entered the camp on September 26, 1863, unaware of the hardships that awaited them. Camp Douglas was built in 1861 on 270 acres near the University of Chicago and the Illinois Central Railroad Yard. It was originally intended to be a training barracks for Union troops, but it was converted to a prisoner of war camp in February 1862.

Conditions were bad from the start but had reached a new low by the time the Plott boys arrived. Though built to house only about four thousand prisoners, more than six thousand were held there by October 1863. Before the war ended in 1865, that number would double, as the prison would eventually house more than twelve thousand Confederate troops. Camp Douglas was not the largest Union prison facility, but it was by far the worst. Much has been written about the horrors of Andersonville, the Confederate prison in Georgia, but Camp Douglas was every bit as bad and probably worse. Noted Civil War historian Dr. John McGlone explains it like this:

> *The tragedy of the much publicized prison at Andersonville was that a war weary Confederate government could not feed, clothe, or provide medical care for its own people, much less enemy prisoners. The shame of Camp Douglas was that the Union government could have provided for their Confederate prisoners, but didn't.*

Not only was the prison terribly overcrowded, but disease was rampant and rations and good medical care were scarce. And it could easily all have been avoided. The Federal government had the resources and at one time even appropriated $20,000 for improvements and supplies for the camp—but the money mysteriously disappeared.

Three months after the Plott brothers arrived, a blizzard set in for days. In January 1864, temperatures dropped to eighteen degrees below zero.

Many Privations to Endure

Many of the men had no coats or blankets and froze to death. Worse yet, a succession of sadistic Union camp commanders authorized brutal treatment and torture of the prisoners. Some of their worst offenses included:

- Hanging prisoners by their thumbs for an hour or more at a time.
- Beating men with belts while they were hung from upper bunks by their feet.
- Regularly putting men in chains attached to a thirty-two-pound cannonball and sentencing them to as many as twenty-one days in a dungeon, with only dirty water and moldy bread for sustenance.
- Stripping troops naked in frigid temperatures and forcing them to sit bare-bottomed in the snow until they froze to it.
- Beating starving prisoners for eating snow.
- Routinely subjecting prisoners to a form of torture that Confederate troops referred to as "riding the mule." In this case, the "mule" was a sharp-edged plank that prisoners were forced to sit astride, suspended above the ground with their hands tied behind them. Union guards often increased the prisoner's suffering by securing a bucket of sand to each of their feet. The guards called this "giving the Rebels a pair of spurs." A specially constructed "mule" was fifteen feet high. One prisoner was forced to ride it for eight hours a day for an entire week in subzero weather.
- Rewarding particularly cruel Union guards for beating, torturing and even shooting prisoners.

When all else failed, the Union wardens cut the already meager prisoner rations in half, increased work details and confiscated warm clothing and blankets. This resulted in hundreds of prisoners dying from diseases like scurvy, dysentery and smallpox, as well as from exposure, hunger and fatigue. Inmates were reduced to eating rats and even a pet dog. One prisoner recalled that "we caught big gray rats and made them into rat pie," while another later remembered what an unknown camp humorist wrote after eating the dog: "For lack of bread the dog is dead, for want of meat the dog was eat."

Imagine what a physical and mental shock this must have been for all these prisoners, but especially for the Plott brothers. For the better part of two decades, the Plott boys had run the ridges of the Great Smoky Mountains hunting bears behind their dogs and living in a virtual wilderness paradise. With every kind of native wild game to hunt and catch, as well as farm-grown beef, chicken, pork and fruits and vegetables, the brothers had always eaten like kings. They had grown into robust and strapping adults who feared no man, and yet now, their lives were resigned to this—a place of misery beyond human comprehension. Surely it could not get any worse. But it did.

Before the end of almost two years of captivity—from late September 1863 to June 26, 1865—Robert Henry Plott was subjected to, or at the very least had witnessed, all of these atrocities and more. But none of his suffering could compare to the agony he felt in 1864 when not one but *both* of his beloved brothers died of smallpox.

Hebron Plott and Leander Plott were buried in an anonymous huge grave outside the camp. The grave was referred to by guards as "the Confederate Mound." With more than six thousand Confederate prisoners eventually entombed there, this would be the largest mass grave *ever* in the recorded history of the *entire* western hemisphere—yet another little-known fact in the horror that was Camp Douglas.

It is difficult to even speculate as to what compelled the Federal wardens to treat prisoners in such a heinous manner. Their sadistic actions are beyond the scope of human understanding and they cannot be explained, excused or rationalized. But at least part of their strategy—if it can be called that—was to demoralize the prisoners to the point that they would swear allegiance to the Union and thus win their release.

Prisoners considered this treason and referred to taking this oath of allegiance as "swallowing the dog." Nevertheless, as their own conditions weakened while their comrades suffered and died around them, many began to consider this a viable option. More than 1,500 prisoners took the oath and won their release or were exchanged for Federal prisoners in 1864. Robert Henry Plott was *not* among them.

Despite what he would later describe in a letter to his parents as "having had many privations to endure," and despite the loss of his two brothers, Robert Plott remained steadfast in his loyalty to the South and refused to "swallow the dog." He would pay a terrible price for his decision.

In September 1864, the prisoners were offered amnesty by swearing allegiance to the Union and joining the Federals in fighting the Indians in the western United States. Many Southerners saw this as a good opportunity for freedom, as they would not have to fight against their own army or return home in disgrace. On September 14, 1864, a large contingent of prisoners took the oath and headed west—but not Plott.

Meanwhile, conditions at Camp Douglas worsened. The winter of 1864–65 was even harsher than the previous year. At least 1,091 men died in four months, the worst loss in the entire Union prison system and equal to

Many Privations to Endure

Andersonville's February through May 1864 body count. Before the end of the war, Camp Douglas would house a grand total of 25,000 Confederate troops and more than 7,500 of them ended up dead or unaccounted for. One out of six prisoners—more than 15 percent—who passed through the gates of Camp Douglas died there. But somehow Robert Henry Plott managed to survive and soldier on.

Plott would later attribute his membership in the Masons and the kindness of fellow Union Masons as a partial reason for his survival. Even in the depths of depravity that was Camp Douglas, some of the Masonic Union guards showed kindness to their captive brothers and occasionally helped them. Plott had joined the Masons shortly before enlisting in the army and he was the second charter member initiated into the Waynesville, North Carolina Masonic Lodge.

As the suffering and death continued, more prisoners chose to swear allegiance to the Union to win their release—and who could blame them? Fifteen hundred took the oath in February 1865 and they continued to leave in huge numbers in the months that followed. It is interesting to note that the real life inspiration of Charles Frazier's novel *Cold Mountain*—W.P. Inman—was probably among this group. He was later killed by the Haywood County Home Guard as he walked home from prison.

The Confederacy surrendered in April and the prison rapidly emptied. By early June, only 1,770 hardcore Rebels were left, all of whom refused to swear allegiance to the Union. Among them was Robert Henry Plott. However, by mid-June 1865, all of the "healthy" prisoners who could walk were released—*except* for Plott.

Perhaps it was retribution for his steadfast loyalty to the South, or maybe it was just an honest mistake. But regardless of the reason, prison authorities refused to release Plott, saying that his records had been lost. In a touching letter to his parents dated June, 15, 1865, Robert Henry Plott wrote in part:

Dear Father and Mother,

I take the present opportunity of writing you a few lines. I am still in prison yet and do not know when I will be released. I would have gotten off tomorrow if my name had been on the record, but by some means it can not be found on the books.

I expect that I shall have to stay here till all the rest of the prisoners have been released. I think though, that I will get out in a week or two. I will be myself going home. I am sorry I did not get off with the rest of the boys. That I can not help.

When I leave this place I expect to take my transportation to Greenville, Tennessee. I will have to walk from there home. I want you to have some clothing made by the time I get home. I want you to wait with patience till I get home. I think it will not be long, though it seems like I have been a prisoner a long time and have had many privations to endure, though I have borne it with all the patience a man could under the present circumstances.

I will close for the present. I am sending these lines by a friend who leaves this place tomorrow.

I remain your affectionate son till death,

Robert H. Plott

Having endured almost two years of imprisonment, Robert Henry Plott was finally granted his freedom on June 26, 1865. More than two months after Lee's surrender at Appomattox, Plott was apparently the very last defiant Rebel prisoner to walk out of Camp Douglas. After losing two brothers and scores of friends and suffering unimaginable cruelty, he was finally headed back to a life of freedom and hunting in the Great Smoky Mountains. Plott boarded a train in Chicago, Illinois, bound for Greeneville, Tennessee. He was a man on a mission.

MAN ON A MISSION

We can only guess what Robert Henry Plott was thinking as his train pulled into Greeneville, Tennessee, in late June 1865. But surely the trip must have been bittersweet. He was returning home alone without his two brothers, in a weakened, penniless state. However, he had to have been excited to still be alive and headed back to his parents and their mountain home. Plott had a lot to think about as he began his journey of more than fifty miles across the Smokies to North Carolina.

Still wearing his dirty, tattered Confederate uniform, he embarked on his trip home a determined man. He vowed that he would not marry or raise a family until he had enough land and money to ensure that they would never go hungry again. Plott wanted to make sure that neither he nor anyone close to him would ever have to suffer as he and his brothers had for the past two years.

We don't know the exact route that he took home, but likely it was on the old wagon road through Cataloochee and over the mountains into what is now Maggie Valley. He surely gained strength as he began to breathe crisp mountain air and to see people and places familiar to him. Just as he had requested, he found a clean set of new garments left for him by his parents on the banks of Jonathan Creek. It was here that he bathed and changed clothes because he did not want his parents to see him in his previous condition. The clear, cold water must have been a pleasant shock to him as he cleaned up and changed into his new clothing. Moreover, he must have been happy, yet sad, to think about the good times he and his late brothers had shared hunting and fishing here as boys.

Robert Henry Plott and wife, the former Martha Moody. *Courtesy of Louise Plott.*

Plott—still not yet twenty-five years of age—undoubtedly returned home a different person. A giant of a man whose already strong will had been hardened in the forges of hell called Camp Douglas, Plott now had a plan. And he wasted no time in executing it.

Man on a Mission

For the next seven years, Robert worked on the family homestead like a man possessed, farming and logging. He saved every penny that he could and gradually began to acquire more land to build his fortune. When he wasn't working, Plott was hunting and training the clan's pack of Plott hounds.

By 1873, Robert Henry Plott was wealthy enough to consider marriage. In January, he married eighteen-year-old Martha Moody. Robert and Martha Plott began their life together in a cabin on upper Jonathan Creek near the original David Plott homestead. By 1874, they had the first of their eleven children—five girls and six boys.

In 1881, Robert cut, sawed and hand-dressed the lumber needed to build a beautiful home for his growing family. President Grover Cleveland appointed Plott postmaster in the community in 1885. He opened the post office in his home and operated it here for the next forty-one years. It would be known simply as "Plott" until October 30, 1926, when the name was changed to Maggie Valley.

Plott had the best of both worlds here. He owned plenty of flat, fertile valley land to raise his family, farm and log. Surrounded by mountain peaks, it was perfect for bear hunting as well as for trying to forget the horrors of war and his imprisonment.

Robert Henry Plott and his daughters at the home he built in 1881. *Courtesy of Louise Plott.*

A pack of Plott dogs at the home of Robert Henry Plott. *Courtesy of Louise Plott.*

Man on a Mission

Robert generally employed traditional bear-hunting methods. He would scout for bear sign and then take his pack out until they found a fresh trail. Plott followed them closely until the bruin was contained (bayed or treed) and killed. However, like many old-time hunters, Plott often allowed his dogs to run loose on his farm, and sometimes he would just drop whatever he was doing and go to them when he heard them strike a bear trail or bay it from miles away.

Back then, hunting was not just a sport; it was more a matter of survival. Dogs were multipurpose free-ranging canines used to hunt game, herd farm animals and protect their owners. As a result, hunters placed an even stronger value on a tenacious dog that would stay with the bear for an extended period of time—and none was better at this than Robert's pack of Plott hounds.

Plott was once awakened shortly after midnight by the sound of his dogs chasing a bear in the nearby mountains. Tired from a hard day's work, he ignored their distant barking and went back to sleep. The next morning as he went about his daily chores, he could tell from the sounds of their voices that his dogs had treed the bruin. But he was too busy the remainder of the day to address it.

At nightfall, the barking continued, and Plott considered going after the bear and his dogs. However, he estimated that the dogs had been at the bear tree for almost twenty-four hours straight and surely would tire and head home before he got there. Instead, he went to bed. Much to his dismay, Robert's determined pack continued to howl throughout that night.

The baying persisted deep into the second day. Finally, irritated but nonetheless proud of his dogs, he grabbed a gun and went after them late that evening. He wasn't going through another sleepless night. Robert climbed the ridge behind his home, where he eventually found his hounds and quickly disposed of the bear. His remarkable canines had stayed at the bear tree containing the bruin for almost forty-eight consecutive hours!

Even by the Plotts' lofty standards, these were exceptional dogs. They were such skillful animals that on a normal hunt they would keep a bear so closely contained that Robert could slip in among them and dispatch the beast with his single-shot "horse" pistol. This was one of the pistols he had captured in the Civil War.

One of Robert Plott's only two surviving granddaughters, eighty-seven-year-old Helen Luckadoo, described her grandfather's dogs: "They were medium height, and thick chested, with shorter ears and legs than your normal hound dog. They were dark brown in color with prominent brindle stripes and weighed no more than sixty pounds. The dogs were

Man on a Mission

exceptionally intelligent and loyal to a fault." The other surviving granddaughter, ninety-three-year-old Carmen Plott, added: "They were beautiful animals, much too pretty to be mean old hunting dogs; they were more like pets to me."

Plott's dogs were exceptionally intelligent. One old-time hunter provided this colorful explanation: "Them dogs is so savvy that if they are still runnin' when hunters leave the woods, they'll check in with the game warden before coming home!"

Robert Henry Plott was an extraordinary hunter, but he was an even better businessman. He accrued a fortune in the cattle and lumber industries. He not only carried on the family tradition of hunting and breeding bear dogs, but he was also the first man in Haywood County to breed Black Angus cattle. His success as a cattleman often resulted in allowing him to combine business with pleasure.

Bears found a convenient food source in the Plott livestock, and the bruins raided the cattle and sheep herds often. The Plott family seldom

A hunter's cabin, similar to Black Camp Gap cabin. *Courtesy of Great Smoky Mountains National Park Archives.*

missed an opportunity to bear hunt, but the fact that the bears were cutting into his profits made Robert Henry even more passionate about the sport. Some of his cattle pastured near Black Camp Gap, just north of Soco Gap on the Haywood–Swain County line. Plott built a cabin here near the mouth of Bunches Creek to house his cattle rangers and to use for a hunting camp. Though it is no longer standing, relatives say that it was a rustic log building with bunk beds, a stone fireplace and a cookstove, with a table and chairs inside.

Black Camp Gap would be the western Haywood County bear-hunting headquarters for Robert, his sons and neighbors for almost fifty years. Not long after the camp was built, it was damaged in a forest fire, charring the logs. Afterward, hunters and herders who stayed there complained about the soot from the walls staining their clothing black—thus earning the name Black Camp Gap. The Blue Ridge Parkway now runs through the property and a National Park Service sign honoring the Plott family and their dogs was later placed south of here. The Park Service paid Robert Plott's heirs twenty dollars an acre for the land in 1939.

Robert was also a charter member of a famous Haywood County hunting club. The organization—founded by Dr. Nick Medford—was formally named the Waynesville Rod and Gun Club. But most locals referred to it simply as the hunting club, or the Waynesville Hunting Club. The clubhouse still stands today in southern Haywood County, above Sunburst near the headwaters of the Pigeon River. The caretaker and game warden for the club was a man named "Moose" Burris. Trout were so plentiful here that Burris sought to "conserve" them by restricting the limit of club members to fifty trout *each* per outing. Robert, and later his sons Cody, Jim, Homer and Hub, would enjoy hunting and fishing here for more than half a century.

As his riches grew, so did his landholdings. By the end of the nineteenth century, Plott was the largest taxpayer in Haywood County and one of its biggest landowners. He owned almost all of what is now Maggie Valley—nearly 3,500 acres—stretching from high on Soco Gap down into the Dellwood community. Robert also invested in or owned several other businesses, including a lumber company, sawmill, hotel and hardware store.

Though by nature a frugal man, Plott rewarded his prosperity by ordering himself an expensive custom-made bear-hunting rifle. Old age and two years in Union captivity had taken a toll on Robert Plott's body. He could no longer follow his dogs quickly to the bears and kill them at close range with a pistol. So he commissioned a top Greenville, South Carolina gun

Man on a Mission

Some members of the Waynesville Rod and Gun Club. Founding member Dr. Nick Medford is in the top row, center, in a long-sleeved plaid shirt. *Courtesy of Steven and Linda Rich.*

maker—probably either Thomas or David Peden—to build him a big bore rifle with extra long-range knockdown power. The gunsmith built the old hunter a .69-caliber rifle that shot a one-ounce ball. Plott supposedly killed several more bears with the weapon.

When he wasn't tending to his various business interests or bear hunting, Plott would ride by horseback to the courthouse in Waynesville. Here he would often sit and read the newspaper aloud to any local folks who wanted to catch up on current events. In his home he kept a well-stocked library of his favorite books, along with a world map where he charted the progress of allied forces during conflicts such as the Spanish-American War and later World War I. Robert was intrigued by the world outside the mountains and he apparently was well-known outside of Haywood County as well.

In about 1905, Plott was asked by President Theodore Roosevelt to host the noted forestry expert Gifford Pinchot in his home. Pinchot was the director of the newly formed United States Forest Service, and he was in the area to explore and write a report on what would later become the Great Smoky Mountains National Park. Roosevelt considered Plott an authority on the region and asked that he assist Pinchot in any way possible. Robert managed to temporarily set aside his strong dislike for both Roosevelt and Pinchot's Republican Party affiliations to honor the president's request. Using Pinchot's research, Roosevelt wrote a report that later inspired Colonel David Chapman to become a park advocate. Chapman, Horace Kephart and Mr. and Mrs. W.P. Willis, among others, led the efforts in campaigning for the eventual formation of the Great Smoky Mountains National Park in 1934.

Robert Henry Plott would not live to see that. He hunted, raised Plott dogs and supervised his various business ventures until his death in 1926 at the age of eighty-six. At the time of his demise, the Plott family had been hunting in the Great Smoky Mountains for almost 125 years. For all his many contributions to mountain hunting culture and history, it is Plott's assistance in the initial formation and preservation of the Great Smoky Mountains National Park that some would consider the most fitting. It is appropriate that a native son to the region would play a role—albeit a small one—in permanently preserving the very same mountains that he had dreamed of returning to while being held a captive of the Federal government.

However, it is possible that his most impressive legacy was not his support of the park or even his amazing rags-to-riches life story. Instead, it was the little-known role he played in perpetuating the Plott family tradition of hunting big game and raising bear dogs in the Great Smoky Mountains. Perhaps more significantly, it was his ability to instill that same love and dedication in four of his sons—the next generation of Smoky Mountain Plott hunters.

THE NEXT GENERATIONS

Robert Henry Plott lived long enough to see most of his children marry and have children of their own. Like his father and grandfather before him, he entrusted some of them with continuing the family history of raising Plott dogs and mastering the art of bear hunting in the Great Smokies. In this case, it was Homer, Jim and particularly Cody and Herbert Plott who were designated to carry this rich tradition deep into the twentieth century. Though little is commonly known about these next generations, their story is nonetheless compelling.

JAMES ROBERT PLOTT

James (Jim) Robert Plott was born in 1879 and took to the woods quickly—so much so that in 1899, at the age of twenty, he headed west to Washington State to log and hunt. Perhaps like his forefathers before him, Jim left simply to find better hunting country. Or maybe he chose to leave simply to be his own man.

Regardless of his reasons, the Pacific Northwest was the preferred destination for many young western North Carolina mountaineers seeking their fortune during that time. Jobs were plentiful in the logging industry and the lumber companies paid a bounty on the many bears that were destroying trees there. A man could make a good living, or at least supplement it, simply by doing what he loved best—hunting. This seemed almost too good to be true for hundreds of eastern hunters and loggers as they would head west to find work for the next sixty years.

It has been speculated, but never substantiated, that Jim Plott was responsible for bringing the first Plott bear dogs to the far West, a place where the breed would later gain international acclaim. However, substantial documentation indicates that it was another Haywood County hunter, Mark Reece, who was responsible for taking Plott hounds to the far West. Reece and his family moved near Darrington, Washington, in 1906 with Plott dogs that they had originally obtained from Montraville Plott.

Jim enjoyed the hunting and logging life in Washington and did well there. It was where he met and married his wife, Mabel Sprinkle. It was also where Jim learned to ice skate, a sport that he enjoyed for the rest of his life. Jim and Mabel Plott returned home to the Great Smoky Mountains in about 1910. Together, they raised five children and were married for more than half a century.

Mabel Plott was a well-known midwife in Maggie Valley. One of the many children she helped deliver was her grandson, James Robert Plott III. The newborn child's mother was having difficulty providing sustenance for her baby due to milk caking in her breasts. Mabel came up with a unique solution to the problem. She instructed Jim to bring some young Plott dog pups in to resolve the issue—and they did. With his mother's milk flowing free, the hungry baby was saved.

Jim and his younger brother Homer made their living by operating a sawmill in Maggie Valley and a lumber company in Waynesville. Their brother Cody would also later join them in the lumber business, appropriately named Plott Brothers Lumber Company. Jim cut and sawed the timber for his family home and built the house himself in 1916. It still stands on Timberline Drive in Maggie Valley. By 1920, he was generating electricity to light the home from his own water-powered gristmill. It was one of the first—if not *the* first—homes in Maggie Valley to have electricity.

He also farmed and occasionally sold Plott dogs. Jim probably did not own Plott hounds while living out west, but he certainly resumed the rich family tradition of hunting and dog breeding when he returned home. Jim McGha recalls getting his first Plott hounds from Jim and Cody Plott in 1939. Plott was an avid bear hunter who never cared much for small game hunting. Relatives say that he was a generous man who always shared the meat from his many bear kills with his neighbors.

The Next Generations

A Plott hound owned by Jim Plott. *Courtesy of James Plott III.*

Jim was a member of a 1939 bear hunting party that proved to be memorable for two reasons. One was the size of the bruin killed—it was a monster. The bear, shot by Joe Parris, not far from Jonathan Creek, weighed almost five hundred pounds. The other reason was that the bear was the exact same animal that had run Little George Plott up a tree in 1937 on an earlier Hazel Creek, North Carolina hunt (see chapter "Little George"). Little George, also in this hunting party, easily identified the beast by the large scar across the bear's nose and chest. Other well-known hunters in this group included Von Plott, Ralph Campbell and Taylor Wilson.

James Plott III shared a humorous story regarding a Jim Plott bear hunt. Farmers in the Maggie Valley area, indeed all around the Smokies, were often plagued with rogue bears killing their livestock. The problem worsened in 1934 with the formation of the Great Smoky Mountains National Park. The new park provided a safe haven for the raiding bruins.

After a bear had killed several of Jim's calves near Wickles Fork, he and some of his neighbors turned their Plott dogs loose on the trail of the beast. Eventually, the hounds ran the bear back into the park. But this time, the infuriated hunters did not stop at the boundary. Instead, they followed the animal into the sanctuary and killed it.

Afterward, Jim and his party were arrested on federal charges and later tried for the crime. The prosecuting attorney called each of the hunters to the stand and chastised them soundly for the killing. He talked down to the mountain men and arrogantly posed this question to them: "You men are a disgrace; as old bear hunters, shouldn't you know better than to do such a terrible thing?" To which Jim and his buddies all answered, "Yes, we are poor old mountain bear hunters, but we will never admit to knowing better."

To the disgust of the lawyer—who had asked them to hand down the most severe penalty possible—the jury instead voted to acquit the hunters.

Another hunting story involving Plott has the makings of an epic frontier tall tale—but in this case, it is believed to be true. Jim and his hounds ran the bear up a deep, dead-end ravine. Jim headed the bruin off on a ridge above the gulch. He spotted a log bridging the chasm and ran out on it to shoot the animal as it ran toward him down below. He squeezed off a shot, but his rifle misfired. Without hesitation, Jim threw the gun aside, leaped off the log onto the back of the bear and killed it with a knife.

If this is true—and I believe that it is—Jim Plott was at least the fourth member of the Plott family to have killed a bear armed only with a knife. But in his case, he evidently was able to make the kill yet walk away with only minor cuts and bruises.

Left to right: Homer, Hub and Jim Plott. *Courtesy of Louise Plott.*

The Next Generations

Aside from his family and bear hunting, there was nothing Jim Plott loved more than dancing and ice skating. He often skated on the millpond behind his home when it froze over in the winter. Jim delighted in gliding gracefully around the ice on the skates he had first purchased while living in Washington. Plott also built a dance hall in front of the gristmill so he would always have a place to dance.

His niece, Helen Luckadoo, remembers her uncle as a fun-loving man who was a superb dancer:

> *As a child it was a great thrill to dance with Uncle Jim. And what a dancer he was! He was so graceful moving across the dance floor. He loved dancing so much that he built his own dance hall behind the family home. There was a stone walkway leading to it. They would host a neighborhood square dance there every Tuesday night and people would come from all around. Those were real good times.*

Jim Plott would continue to enjoy those good times for the remainder of his life. He danced, skated, hunted and raised Plott dogs until shortly before his death in 1967 at the age of eighty-eight.

HENRY HOMER PLOTT

Homer Plott spent a good deal of his youth perfecting his hunting skills under the tutelage of his older brothers and father. When he wasn't hunting or working on the family farm, he was playing baseball. Homer stood six feet and four inches tall, and in his late teens he developed into an over-powering left-handed pitcher. He played professional baseball in the Midwestern minor leagues in about 1908. Prior to that, Homer went to school at Tusculum College in Greeneville, Tennessee. But he found that he preferred the night life to schoolwork and eventually dropped out. Homer remained there almost a year, working and partying. He pretended to still be in school rather than going back home and risking the ire of his father, Robert Henry.

After mustering the courage to return home, he joined the family lumber business, married and had a family of his own. Homer's daughter, Carmen Plott, remembers her father as a man who loved to bear hunt and enjoy life. She also recalled that he took good care of his Plott hunting dogs:

He never kept a lot of dogs—usually only two or three, never more than four—and he often let them run loose. He took real good care of them. One of his favorites was a female dog—I can't remember her name. She took sick a couple days before bear-hunting season opened and he stayed up around the clock attending to her. But she died anyway on the day the season started. He was real sad about that. We baked cakes of dog bread to feed our dogs. This was coarse ground cornmeal baked into round cakes, usually in a skillet. They seemed to like it a lot.

Regarding the disposition of the dogs, she continued: "They were generally friendly. But one night I came home and surprised one of them. He thought I was an intruder and he about ate me up until I managed to get in the house."

Homer was supposedly a crack shot, and he was undoubtedly quick witted. He favored light-caliber rifles like a .22 to hunt with. A friend once commented that it was not safe for him to hunt bear with such a small-bore gun. Homer replied with a grin: "It is not risky, as long as you can shoot the bear in the left eye every time!"

The 1941 bear hunt with seven Plott relatives. *Front row, left to right*: John A. Plott, Big George Plott, Homer Plott and Cody Plott. *Back row, left to right*: Little George Plott, Herbert Plott Jr. and Von Plott. *Courtesy of Wayne Battle.*

The Next Generations

Despite being relatively unknown today, Homer and his brother Cody Plott participated in one of the most famous bear hunts ever conducted in the Great Smoky Mountains. And it was the *only* documented hunt in which seven members of the famous Plott family hunted together. In December 1941, an all-star roster of hunters gathered at the Hazel Creek, North Carolina "clubhouse" for a bear hunt. The group included both Cody and Homer Plott and their nephew, Herbert Plott Jr. They were joined by John A. Plott, his son "Little George" and John's brothers Von and Big George. Herbert Jr., Little George and Big George were all home on leave from military service in World War II.

In addition to the seven members of the Plott clan, other hunters on this outing included seventy-year-old Mark Cathey, Jim and Oliver Laws, Taylor Wilson, Wince Cable, Bill Wiggins, Ronald Aldridge and Ray Wright. These mountain hunting icons were serving as guides for a host of "outlander" visitors that included, among others, Senator William Smathers of New Jersey. The guides helped their big-city clients harvest three big bears—all over three hundred pounds—on the trip.

The Plott family. *Bottom row, left to right*: Jim Plott, Mrs. Martha Plott and Minnie Plott. *Top row, left to right*: Cody Plott, Roy Plott, Homer Plott, Herbert Plott and David Plott. *Courtesy of Wayne Battle.*

The Plott brothers contributed to the family hunting tradition and to mountain cultural history as well. Homer's daughter Carmen Plott and her cousins Gertrude Plott (Jim's daughter), Josephine Plott (Cody's daughter) and Herbert Plott Jr. and his sister Evelyn (Hub's children) were all members of the famous Soco Gap Square Dance Team. This talented group toured the United States and entertained President Franklin Roosevelt and his wife Eleanor at the White House in 1939. The Roosevelts' special guests were King George and Queen Elizabeth of England.

When asked in the winter of 2009 about that trip, Carmen Plott said, "That King sure was a good-looking man!" Still feisty, but bedridden at age ninety-three, Carmen Plott retains the colorful spirit of her late father Homer. Like his brother Jim, Homer Plott lived to the ripe old age of eighty-eight. He died in 1973.

Grover Cleveland Plott

Robert Henry Plott was so elated that a Democrat was finally going to be president that he named his third son after the candidate. Grover Cleveland Plott was born on April 20, 1884, but he soon acquired the nickname of Cody. It was name fitting of an accomplished outdoorsman, and he was seldom called anything else for the remainder of his life.

Cody recalled that he began hunting and fishing as soon as he was big enough "to tote a gun and pole." As a small boy, he raised a chicken and sold it to the owner of the Dellwood General Store to buy his first box of ammunition. Like his brothers and father, Cody embraced the life of a woodsman, but he was also a good student. He especially loved American frontier history and closely studied the legends behind the family Plott hound. Both Cody and his cousin Samuel Plott would eventually become family historians on the breed, and they were best friends. Cody was later the best man at Sam's wedding.

Many Plott dog historians believe that it was Montraville Plott who first crossed his family dogs to some leopard hounds from Rabun Gap, Georgia, in the late 1800s. Cody, however, maintained that it was Henry Plott who initially crossed the dogs with some hounds from Tocoa, Georgia, in the early 1800s. Cody also felt strongly that the original Plott dog was more of a cur and that the hound bloodlines were introduced to give the dogs more tongue (loud bark) and a keener nose.

The Next Generations

By the time he graduated from high school, there few better woodsmen in Haywood County than Cody Plott. Though proud of his son's hunting skills, his father needed educated help running his various business ventures. So Robert Henry sent both Cody and Homer off to college at Tusculum. Cody stayed there for three years and did well, but he returned home in about 1909 to assist his father.

Under the watchful eye of Robert Henry, Cody began to manage his father's businesses. By 1915, Cody, Homer and Jim Plott were all married and had started families of their own. Cody and Homer moved into the town of Waynesville and lived next door to each other. Cody managed the family hardware store and hotel there while Jim and Homer took care of the lumber business.

Living in town never interfered with Cody's bear hunting. He still managed to hit the woods frequently. Eighty-seven-year-old Helen Luckadoo, Cody's last surviving child, remembers her father returning from bear hunting: "He almost always brought bear meat home and he would often bring the carcass in the house and butcher it on the kitchen table. Daddy cooked some bear meat for me one time; I took one bite and I never ate it again."

Helen laughed and then added these comments:

> *When I was about sixteen years old, my boyfriend Jack and I were swinging on the front porch swing when Daddy returned from a hunt. As usual, he had killed a bear and he brought it in the kitchen to dress it. Jack was already nervous about being there and it only got worse when Daddy drove up with a dead bear and carrying a rifle. While Daddy was butchering the bear, his rifle somehow accidentally went off. The loud shot about scared Jack to death and he jumped from the porch and hit the ground running. He never turned around once!*

Maybe the shot was an accident, but it seems more likely to have been a trick to scare his daughter's first suitor. It is difficult to imagine such an accomplished hunter as Cody Plott having this sort of mishap in his home. But whether accident or prank, it is nonetheless a good story. Cody instilled that same sense of humor and adventure into all his children—particularly his daughter Helen, who later served as a member of the U.S. Navy WAVES in World War II.

Living in town prevented Cody from keeping a pack of Plott dogs there. However, he still owned several Plott hounds and kept them at his brother Jim's home in Maggie Valley. He also would later keep some hunting dogs with his baby brother Hub. But it was a pet mutt that his daughter Helen remembers best. She said that the animal was a mixed-breed mongrel and that it was extremely loyal to her father. The dog would ride on the roof of Cody's car as he drove to the Sloan-Plott Hardware Store in downtown Waynesville. The faithful cur would sleep on the hood of the car all day as it waited for Cody to take him back home at night.

Cody eventually closed the hardware store and for several years served as chairman of the Haywood County Board of Education. But it was in 1934 that Cody Plott found his true calling as a state wildlife official. He was hired as the Haywood County game warden, and there were few men better suited for the job. Cody served in this capacity for eleven years. He was known as a strict but fair law officer.

Plott recalled that during his first few years on the job, the county was a rough and rowdy place. In 1938 alone, Cody had eighty-four arrests and eighty-one of them resulted in convictions. As time went on, citizens came to better respect both the wildlife laws and Cody Plott. Though threatened a few times, Plott said that he never had any real trouble with any of his arrests. But in a 1941 newspaper interview, he humbly described a potentially dangerous showdown that turned out to be humorous:

> *Only one violator has ever given me any real trouble since I have been in office, and he was hunting out of season. When I told him that I would have to take him in he replied that it will take a real man to do that. I then told him that I was man enough to do it and he dropped his gun and fell to the ground. I simply picked him up and carried him to the car without further ado.*

During the course of his career as a wildlife officer, Plott sold $27,500 worth of fishing licenses and $25,000 worth of hunting licenses, many of them to residents from outside the county and state. Plott later stated in 1945 that he had sold licenses to men and women from the age of sixteen to eighty-six. One of these licenses was sold to Isaiah Kidd.

I mentioned in my first book that Cody Plott first met Isaiah Kidd in 1927, but the date was more likely around 1935. Kidd, a West Virginia sheriff, had first seen Plott dogs owned by North Carolina loggers working near his home in the 1920s. He took a hunting vacation to western North Carolina about 1935 and met Cody Plott here. It was Cody who provided Kidd with a history of the breed and introduced him to various Plott family members to obtain breeding stock. The meeting would prove to be monumental in Plott dog history. Over the next thirty plus years—until his death in 1967—Isaiah Kidd would develop his own strain of Plott dogs and become one of the breed's most renowned contributors.

At about this same time, a rogue bear known as Honest John was terrorizing Smoky Mountain farms. The bear was said to weigh close to eight hundred pounds, far bigger than any bruin ever seen before in the region. His paw prints were distinct in that they were bigger than a man's hat and one rear paw was missing three toes lost previously in a trap. The beast possessed unusual stamina. For more than a decade—from the late 1920s to the early 1940s, perhaps longer—the bear was spotted attacking farm animals in almost every county in far western North Carolina. Honest John earned his nickname due to the fact that he killed only to eat. The monster bruin would raid a farm, taking exactly what he needed and nothing more, while leaving the remainder of the livestock untouched.

Though he was well respected by hunters and farmers alike, both groups nonetheless wanted Honest John dead. A host of hunters whose names read like a Smoky Mountain Hunting Hall of Fame all failed at

Little George and Cody Plott measuring the track of "Honest John." *Courtesy of Wayne Battle.*

Plott pups owned by Cody and Jim Plott. *Courtesy of Wayne Battle.*

The Next Generations

the task. Cody Plott and Little George Plott were among this group. Both men hunted Honest John often, particularly in the Caney Fork area of Jackson County, North Carolina. They are pictured in 1940 accompanied by two of their dogs measuring Honest John's huge track with Cody's game warden hat.

Outdoor Life writer Lee Crutchfield Jr. wrote that Honest John was finally killed by Enoch Tate near Grandfather Mountain in the late 1940s. Other sportsmen maintain that even Honest John would not range that far from his native Smokies. They think that the rogue bruin was never killed and died eventually of old age. However, recent evidence has surfaced that Floyd Rich—whom we will profile in later chapters—*may* have killed Honest John in 1940.

In the early 1940s, legend has it that Cody Plott inadvertently played a part in a "miraculous healing." A local hunter had a full-grown bear that he had raised from a cub. Though harmless, the bear weighed over three hundred pounds and sometimes was hired out to lay down track for hunters to train their hounds. To make sure the bear was not injured by trigger-happy neighbors or by the dogs, Plott was called in to supervise the training.

As usual, the plan was for the bruin to run a few miles to an appointed area and climb a tree. Upon their arrival, hunters would contain their hounds at the bear tree. The bear's owner would then take it safely back home. However, this time the plan went awry as the animal took an unexpected detour and headed straight for an inhabited house. A supposedly crippled man—who for years had drawn government disability checks for his alleged infirmity—was sleeping inside while a pot of beans cooled on the stove.

The man awoke to find the bear snacking on the beans just as two young Plott dogs stormed into the cabin in hot pursuit. Amidst the chaos, the "crippled" man emerged from his home wearing only a nightshirt and ran full-bore for nearly a mile before finally stopping at a neighbor's homestead.

All in all, it had been a successful day. The dogs got in some training. The bear got some exercise and a tasty meal before returning home unharmed. A man was "miraculously healed," resulting in a significant savings to local taxpayers. And Cody got to see it all.

Declining health forced Cody Plott to retire as a game warden after eleven years on the job in 1945. In an interview shortly before his retirement, Plott stated that he was born for the job and regretted having to leave it. He also lamented the declining standards of many bear hunters of that era:

The Next Generations

Our bear hunters are falling off. I mean real bear hunters. Most of them today fall short of the standards set by the old timers. Some of them are combining a hunting trip with too much liquor. Many a good bear hunt has been ruined by too much drinking. Hunting and fishing are like a lot of other things; it takes a sober man to do a good job.

In his later years, Cody Plott spent a great deal of time researching Plott dog history and corresponding with Plott hunters and breeders from around the world. He kept detailed records of this correspondence, as well as a lineage of the family dogs. In addition, Plott kept a meticulous journal of all his hunting trips and activities while working as a game warden. Unfortunately, to date, those records remain lost.

But for all of Cody Plott's achievements, it is the impression that he left on a child—his grandson, Wayne Battle—that is perhaps most impressive.

Wayne Battle is today a retired surgeon and master bear hunter living in Johnson City, Tennessee. Battle's mother, Anna Jean, was the daughter of Cody Plott, and his father, James Madison Battle, descended from some of the earliest settlers in Haywood County. Wayne's father is named after his great-great-Uncle James Battle, who was the first white child born in Waynesville in 1811. So Dr. Battle gets his love of the outdoors and mountain history honestly.

Battle affectionately remembers his grandfather Cody Plott:

By the time I was four years old, his impact on my life had been tremendous. He instilled in me the passion for hunting, history and firearms that still burns in me today. I knew how to load a muzzleloading pistol or rifle before I was five years old. Grandpa taught me how to survive outdoors, how to hunt, how to respect firearms—they aren't toys.

He paused to reflect a moment before continuing:

He had an old 1941 Ford. It was white. As we drove through the Pigeon Valley heading to the headwaters of the Pigeon River, he would patiently point out old log cabins and Indian sites and tell me the stories behind them. He told me stories about Daniel Boone and Davey Crockett, as well as tales about our own Plott relatives. I remember the time he told me the story about the Lost Colony. I hung on to every word. I can still hear his voice clearly even today.

Cody Plott and family. *Courtesy of Wayne Battle.*

The Next Generations

After modestly recalling his own career achievements as a field surgeon in Vietnam, and later as a doctor in east Tennessee, Battle elaborated further on his appreciation for his family, particularly his parents and his grandfather Cody:

> *More importantly he* [Cody] *instilled in me, and my mother before me, a respect and compassion for other people. I remember once my mother told me some children had made fun of a poor local family, the Turpins. Both my grandfather and my mother sternly admonished them, saying, "Don't ever look down on the Turpins! Mrs. Turpin hoed fields and harvested crops for us while our men were gone during the Civil War. We wouldn't have survived without her." My mother was a remarkable woman and my grandfather taught us both a lot. Much of the success I have enjoyed in my life can be attributed to lessons taught to me by my grandfather Cody, as well as my mother Anna, and my father James.*

Cody Plott's life was cut short at the age of sixty-four in 1948. But he left an impressive hunting and personal legacy that still survives today in the twenty-first century.

As the 2008 bear hunting season came to an end, Wayne Battle and friends had legally harvested thirty-eight bears with their vintage hunting weapons and Plott dogs in east Tennessee. Battle considers it an honor to maintain a family hunting tradition that has continued for more than two and a half centuries. He carries the hunting torch for his grandfather Cody Plott more than sixty years after his death. Cody and his brothers would undoubtedly be proud. And none would be prouder than their baby brother, Herbert Plott.

Herbert Moore Plott

Herbert Moore Plott, better known as "Hub," was the last male child of Robert Henry and Martha Plott. Hub was born in 1893. With five older brothers and his father Robert to mentor him, he had no shortage of teachers. The boy enjoyed an idyllic childhood, working, playing, hunting and, most importantly, *learning*. While he did well in school, it was the college of the great outdoors in which the lad truly excelled. Hub was like a sponge, soaking up and retaining every bit of knowledge available to him regarding hunting, trapping, farming, carpentry, blacksmithing, animal husbandry and living a life totally in tune with nature.

Marty Plott Moody remembers her grandfather Hub's uncanny ability to read natural signs and that he could predict the weather better than a trained meteorologist. She wrote in 1976:

> *My grandfather was familiar with the signs of nature and signs of the weather. He could predict snow a week in advance. His most amusing and most accurate forecast came from a train whistle. He always said that if the sound of the evening train whistle crossing Balsam Gap carried over into Maggie Valley it would snow. And it did.*

Hub's daughter-in-law, eighty-eight-year-old Louise Plott, echoed these comments. She said in 2009 that Hub would use the mountain behind his home as a reference point to determine the position of storm clouds to predict rain. By studying the size and color of the cloud, as well as its location in regard to the mountaintop, Hub could not only accurately predict a storm, but also exactly when it would occur.

As he grew into manhood, Hub seemed to combine all the best qualities of his brothers and parents. He was a tall, lean, quick-witted, hardworking young man with a keen sense of humor. The youngster possessed a gentle but firm demeanor that projected an aura of calm strength. In some ways, Plott was a throwback to an earlier frontier era when a man had to be truly self-sufficient to survive—and Hub held steadfast to the old-time ways.

Unlike his brothers Jim and Homer, Hub was never interested in living or even traveling anywhere else—and he seldom did. During the course of his long and productive life, Hub Plott never traveled more than two hundred miles away from his home in the Great Smoky Mountains. It was where he was meant to be.

All that was missing was a wife. Hub found his soul mate in 1916 when he married Nannie Campbell. Like Hub, Nannie was extremely intelligent and resourceful. Together they raised three children—Herbert Jr., Evelyn and John D. They also cared for Hub's parents until Robert's death in 1926 and Martha's passing in 1952. The couple ran the Plott post office in their home until 1926 and lived there the remainder of their lives. Moreover, they consistently demonstrated an ability to live well off the land, just as their ancestors before them had done for almost two centuries.

Hub had a blacksmith shop and shod his own horses. Nannie spun cloth from an antique spinning wheel and made clothing. They worked as a team in the family tobacco and cornfields and apple orchards. Hub continued his father's tradition of raising Black Angus cattle, hogs and Plott bear dogs as well. He ground cornmeal and cured country hams. Nannie, meanwhile, cooked, milked the cows, made butter and maintained a bountiful garden, from which she canned vegetables for the winter. As their children got older, the kids helped their parents with the chores. Even during the Great Depression, there was plenty of hard work but few hard times on the Plott farm.

In late 1929, Hub was unable to hunt or work much on the farm due to a severe case of pneumonia. Not one to sit around, the ingenious mountaineer decided to build a water wheel to generate electricity for his home. Without technical training, Plott was nevertheless as skillful as the best trained engineer. He forged many of the parts needed in his blacksmith shop and cut the sheet metal for the wheel with a hammer and chisel. The sheet metal required numerous perfectly aligned holes for the rivets. Using just a mallet and nail to make the holes, as well as a steady eye to measure them, only one of the three thousand holes was out of sync! The end result was a personal power plant that produced electricity for the Plott family for twenty years. Mrs. Louise Plott remembers that the lights in the home would sometimes dim and brighten depending on the ebb and flow of the water pressure to the wheel. But she adds with a chuckle, "They had electricity in a time when few others did."

Despite all the work involved on the farm, Hub always made time to bear hunt. This was partly for his personal enjoyment and partly to keep the bruins from killing his livestock. Like his forefathers before him, Hub was an excellent hunter, but he was also a well-known trapper. He owned and bred some outstanding hunting dogs. Hub's dogs generally were dark

Hub Plott farm, early 1930s. *Courtesy of Louise Plott.*

Hub Plott and one of his favorite dogs, Rattler. *Courtesy of David Plott and Marti Moody.*

brindle-colored dogs and they had shorter legs and ears, a thicker chest and a blockier head than some Plott hounds. But they shared the same tenacious grit and were exceptionally aggressive. Two of his all-time favorite hunting dogs were a female named Queen and a male called Rattler. Rattler was known to be especially loyal to Hub and was renowned as a fierce bear hound. But Charles Gantte believes that another one of Hub's dogs was even tougher than Rattler.

Gantte developed his own well-known strain of Plott dogs and is recognized as an expert on the breed. As a young man, he hunted with Hub in the Big Bend of the Pigeon River near Waterville, North Carolina. Gantte said that

The Next Generations

Plott had a ferocious catch dog named Leroy. The hound was so surly that Hub was forced to build a special screened-in cage to keep Leroy separate from the other dogs in his truck. The dog was extremely loyal to Hub. No one else could touch him. Charles recalled that Plott once told him with a laugh, "Leroy is my catch dog, my bear fighting dog, he will take the fight to a bear or hog. And he's also real mean, you better not get close to him!"

Hub's grandson, David Plott, says that his grandfather kept a muzzle on another of his dogs to keep it from biting the lad. David added that the canine was so mean that Hub finally quit using it to bear hunt because it was just *too* aggressive. Hub was afraid that the dog would be killed. He later sent the hound to his son, Hub Jr., to hunt hogs in South Carolina.

Ninety-year-old Maggie Valley historian Charlie Clement, a fine hunter himself, remembers these early Plott dogs this way: "They were great dogs, one-man dogs, loyal only to their owner, but boy, were they mean! Most of the time you could not even let them hunt with, or get near, other dogs or else they would tear them up and try and eat them."

As far as we know, Hub kept no record of the many bears that he and his dogs harvested. Like most great hunters, he enjoyed the thrill of the chase and the fellowship of the hunt much more than the killing. Plott told his daughter-in-law Louise that some of his best times were spent in hunting

Hub Plott's dog, Queen. *Courtesy of David Plott.*

A 1960 hunting party. Hub Plott is on the far right, with Plott's Boss and Plott's Jug. *Courtesy of Nancy Moody and Louise Plott.*

camps with friends and family. Louise Plott remembers visiting the rustic Black Camp Gap in the early 1940s and how Hub told her that hunters would often camp there for weeks at a time. Hub explained to her how the hunters amused themselves at night by telling tall tales about previous hunts and good times shared together as boys. They also enjoyed playing pranks on one another, such as cutting the shirttail off any newcomer to the camp. And they often sang songs. When told by Louise that she would have liked to have heard their singing, Hub replied: "Believe me, you would not have wanted to hear us sing, because it was really bad. I mean awful. We couldn't sing a lick. Sometimes the words made no sense at all either, or they were kind of bad, but we enjoyed it."

Hub recalled that on one hunt a big bear quickly turned the tables on one of his buddies, and the hunter became the hunted. The men were hunting out of their Black Camp Gap headquarters when they struck a bear trail near the headwaters of Bunches Creek. The race was on as Hub heard his dogs bay the bear up ahead. His friend, who was acting as a stander on the ridge above the creek, dropped down the slope to shoot the bear. As he was aiming his rifle, the angry animal jumped from the tree, leaped over the dogs and hit the ground running. The bear galloped straight for the hunter with a pack of Plott dogs at its heels.

The Next Generations

The hunter turned and ran frantically back to Bunches Creek, where Hub was preparing to cross the stream. Hub said that the man was "almost walking on water" as the bear chased him into the creek. He added that it would have been comical had it not been so dangerous. Luckily, Hub was there and shot the bear as it closed in for the kill. The man was unhurt, but he was teased about his ability to walk on water for years to come.

We don't know for sure what gun Hub used to make that lifesaving shot. But, in keeping with his traditional old-time beliefs, Plott usually chose a hunting rifle or pistol from the arsenal of vintage black powder weapons that he had inherited from his father, Robert Henry. He had two Civil War–era pistols, a .32-caliber muzzleloading rifle for small game hunting, along with two big-bore muzzleloaders—a .50-caliber rifle and .69-caliber rifle—used for bear hunting. The .32-caliber rifle dates back to the 1830s and the .50-caliber rifle was built in the late eighteenth century. The .69-caliber rifle was the custom-built gun that Robert Henry bought in the late 1800s. With the exception of the .69-caliber rifle, all of these weapons remain in the Plott family today.

Marty Plott Moody remembers watching her grandfather Hub make bullets for his various muzzleloading guns. He would carefully melt lead bars and pour it into ball-shaped molds of the appropriate-sized caliber to

A .32-caliber muzzleloading rifle (top) and a .50-caliber muzzleloading rifle, owned by David, Robert Henry and Herbert Plott, with accoutrements. *Courtesy of Shane Plott.*

Hub Plott's shot bag, powder horn and bullet mold for his muzzleloading weapons. *Courtesy of Shane Plott.*

The Next Generations

produce "bullets." The little girl was fascinated by his manual dexterity and his careful attention to detail. This method of producing bullets or rifle balls dates back to the invention of the first muzzleloading weapons. Hub was carrying on a tradition that began in the early 1700s when the earliest white hunters first visited the Great Smoky Mountains.

Herbert wasn't the only one in the family who was a crack shot. Nannie Plott was also a skilled sharpshooter. Though she had no time for big game hunting, she often killed varmints that raided the family henhouses and gardens. Nannie kept a single-shot .22-caliber rifle handy in the kitchen, and she was quick to use it.

Hub was always looking for ways to improve his dogs. He once had a large bear cub that was used to train his Plott pups. He had brought the baby bear back to his farm after finding it alone and injured in the woods. Plott nursed the animal back to health and it became something of a family pet. The pups would chase and tree the young bruin, but Hub was careful never to let the dogs or the bear hurt one another. Eventually, the bear was returned to the wild unharmed.

There was no food that Hub Plott enjoyed more than bear meat. Herbert Plott Jr. first brought his bride Louise home to visit his parents in October 1942. Bear meat was on the dinner menu, and Hub told his new daughter-in-law, "If you are going to be a Plott, you have to eat bear meat." He then carved Louise off a hunk. She reluctantly sampled it and chewed it slowly, describing it like this:

> *It actually tasted really good. Nannie was a great cook. But the more that I chewed it, the more I thought about what it actually was—a bear. I just could not get past that. Finally I had to spit it out. Hub laughed at me and said that he doubted I would ever make it as a Plott. But I smiled back and said, "I may not be a Plott, but I have the Plott name now and that is good enough."*

Hub agreed, and from that point forward he got along famously with his new daughter-in-law. As much as Hub enjoyed bear, he admitted to Louise that there were some parts of a bruin that he refused to eat: "Some parts of a bear aren't fit to eat and I just throw those parts away. But I can't tell you exactly which parts, because some people like to eat them and I don't want to hurt their feelings or embarrass you in describing the parts."

Hub Plott proudly perpetuated the family Plott dog legacy. Like his brother Cody, Hub also contributed to the history of the Plott hound by his friendship with other breed icons. Most Plott canine historians consider John A. Plott, his brother Von, Taylor Crockett, Isaiah Kidd and Gola Ferguson to be the most influential figures in modern-day Plott dog history. They are often referred to as "the Big Five." Many experts feel that Hub Plott should be added to this elite group.

Hub was related to Von and John Plott and was good friends with Taylor Crockett. But he was an especially close friend to Gola Ferguson. David Plott remembers Hub taking him to Ferguson's home as a child. It was here that the lad first saw Ferguson's famous Plott dogs and his homemade fiddles.

Ferguson was an accomplished luthier and bear hunter. He was a man of many talents—a renaissance man of sorts. During the course of his career, he was a farmer, carpenter, surveyor, schoolteacher, county sheriff, treasurer and school principal. Gola was renowned as a colorful storyteller and orator. He even ran for Congress in 1942.

But for all of Ferguson's well-deserved accolades, it was the development of his own strain of Plott hound that made him famous. Ferguson had obtained his original breeding stock from the Plott family in the early 1900s. He later added some Blevins, Cable and Abel bloodlines to his mix to achieve the Ferguson-Plott dog strain. Of the nearly one hundred Plott dogs first registered in 1946 with the United Kennel Club, eighty or more of them originated from two of Ferguson's legendary Plott hounds—Boss and Tige.

Breed experts Charles Gantte and John Jackson maintain that Hub Plott's dogs had a strong infusion of Ferguson bloodlines. With foundation stock from his father's dogs combined with his best friend Gola Ferguson's hounds, Hub Plott's dogs were second to none. But unlike his more famous friends and relatives, his dogs were not as well known and never received their just recognition. Hub cared little for pedigree papers or registering dogs. Like most old-time hunters, the end result was all that mattered. Bear dogs were proven in the woods, on the hunting trail, not on paper. So too were the real hunters—and Ferguson and Plott were two of the best who ever lived in the Great Smoky Mountains.

Plott and Ferguson also shared another trait—they both possessed a wicked sense of humor. There was nothing they loved more than a good joke. Taylor Crockett once said that humorist Will Rogers had nothing on Gola Ferguson. By most accounts, Hub Plott more than held his own with Ferguson.

I have heard several humorous anecdotes about Ferguson and Plott. The best story is about a bet they supposedly once had with a local fiddle player. However, the story is somewhat controversial in that there are two, perhaps three, versions of the tale. In one version, it is Hub Plott and Gola Ferguson who had a wager with the musician. The other version identifies Von Plott and Ferguson as the culprits. Another yarn maintains that both Von and Hub Plott were in on the bet with Ferguson. Considering the various sources of the story and the close friendship between Ferguson and Hub, I think it is likely that Hub Plott was the Plott clan member involved, or at the very least was present with Von—but I could be wrong. Either way, it is a story worth telling.

Ferguson and Plott had returned from a two-day hunt, in which they had harvested two bears. They stopped at Ferguson's home to rest, skin the bears and feed and water their dogs. As the hunters relaxed a bit before starting their chores, they were approached by a local roving fiddle player named Charlie Crisp. The musician was said to be something of a smart aleck, but he was a superb musician. Ferguson later described Charlie as having the ability "to make notes that could split an atom and charm snakes." Charlie asked Ferguson and Plott if they wanted to hear a song or two. No one enjoyed good music more than Hub and Gola, so they encouraged the troubadour to saw off a few tunes.

The fiddler later implored the two nimrods to make a bet with him. Both hunters were tired and refused the offer. They had no time for the man's foolishness. But Charlie crossed the line when he insulted their dogs. The mountain minstrel supposedly eyed the weary Plott hounds and said, "Them is about the sorriest-looking dogs that I have ever seen. Laying around, all lazy like, you can't tell me them dogs would fight a bear—they are too scrawny and too lazy. Why, if they even saw a bear, they'd run like hell to get away from it."

The musician now had Plott's and Ferguson's full attention. He hesitated a bit and then added, "I'll tell you what, let's make a little bet. Do you have a bear hide around here anywhere?"

Ferguson acknowledged that he did and the man continued: "Well, then, you go and get that hide, tie it on me and I will bet you five dollars that I can act just like a bear, crawl up to them dogs, slap the hell out them and they will run away. I never seen a dog yet that I couldn't back down; I hate them all."

Plott and Ferguson at first refused and told the man that he better go home before he got hurt. The fiddler replied that they better worry about their dogs getting hurt, not him. Charlie then added insult to injury when he asked the hunters to promise not to get mad if he hurt their dogs. That was the last straw. Hub and Gola smiled at each other and happily took the bet.

They secured a bear hide to the man and watched as he hunkered toward the dogs. The hounds quietly watched him approach, not even bothering to get up. As the musician got closer, he rose up, let out a shout and charged the exhausted dogs. He attempted a swat at the closest canine as the other hounds slowly stood up.

In a split second, the dogs tore into the man. Several latched onto the bear hide while others bit and snarled at him. The joke was now on the troubadour as the hounds swarmed over him. Plott and Ferguson watched in amusement. They knew that their dogs were tied and that the man could easily roll out of danger no worse for the wear. The loudmouth would learn a good lesson with only a few nips and scratches to go along with his bruised ego.

Unfortunately for the fiddler, two of the dogs broke free. Charlie screamed as he rolled away from the tied dogs with the bear hide torn off him. But the two unchained canines were fiercely growling and firmly attached to his clothing. Gola and Hub, realizing the problem, quickly rushed to his aid, but not before one of the dogs—a six-month-old pup named Jap—had locked onto the fiddle player's crotch and nearly castrated him.

Hub secured the dogs, and Gola rushed the man into his house to doctor him. Luckily, the musician recovered and later paid his bet. But it ended up costing Gola more than his winning portion of the wager, as the injured fiddler spent the next two weeks in the Ferguson home recuperating from his wounds. Needless to say, the minstrel never doubted Plott dogs again. And the pup, Jap, who wounded Charlie would go on to be one of Ferguson's most famous hunting dogs. Gola later remembered Jap: "He was one of the craftiest hunters that I have ever seen. For bear he was a one-man army. By the time he was a year old he had been on four bear kills. He was my choice of all the hunting dogs I have ever seen."

Gola Ferguson and Hub Plott were like brothers. When Ferguson died in 1962, the elderly hunter left almost his entire pack of Plott hounds to his best friend Hub Plott. It was a final fitting tribute from one master hunter to another.

Hub Plott was proud to continue the lessons instilled in him by his father—a passion for family, the mountains, bear hunting, Plott dogs and living in harmony with nature. Hub clearly exemplified those virtues throughout his life. So, too, did his brothers.

Herbert "Hub" Plott died in 1973 at the age of eighty. Hub's widow, Nannie Plott, continued the old-time ways and carefully preserved Plott family history until her death in 1992. At the time of Hub Plott's passing, the "other Plott boys" had hunted in the Great Smoky Mountains for almost a century and a half, and the Plott family as a whole had hunted in Haywood County for nearly 175 years.

Gola Ferguson and his dog Jap. *Plott Family Collection*.

The Next Generations

Hub and Nannie Plott. *Courtesy of Louise Plott.*

Today, more than two and a half centuries after the Plott clan first brought their legendary dogs to America, Wayne Battle, Bart Campbell, Danny Hooper, Bob Plott and other family members continue the Plott legacy of hunting with their Plott hounds in the Great Smoky Mountains. The "other Plott boys" undoubtedly would be proud to see their family traditions still alive and well in the twenty-first century.

But I suspect that the "other Plott boys" would be even prouder of their cousin—master hunter and soldier Captain George Ellis Plott. Because the story of "Little George" Plott is the stuff of which legends are made.

LITTLE GEORGE

John Amos Plott, the son of Montraville Plott, and his wife, the former Harriet Winchester, left their Haywood County home in the early 1900s and spent almost a decade working in Texas and Kansas. The couple had both of their children while living in Wichita, Kansas. Grace was born in 1907 and George Ellis was born in 1912. By 1920, John had moved his young family back to the mountains of western North Carolina. And it proved to be perfect timing for George Plott.

The old adage "being in the right place at the right time" certainly applied to the formative years and young adult life of George Ellis Plott. By the time he first came to Plott Creek in 1920, his family had been hunting in the Great Smoky Mountains for more than a century. Little George Plott spent the best years of his life in the Great Smoky Mountains. He was greatly influenced by his father John, as well as his uncles—Vaughn (Von), George and Samuel Plott. He was dubbed "Little" George so as to avoid confusion with his Uncle "Big" George Plott, who lived nearby. "Big" George was a career military man who served with distinction in the U.S. Army in three major conflicts—the border war with Mexican revolutionary Pancho Villa in 1916, World War I in France in 1918 and, still later, in World War II. Samuel Plott also served on the border fighting Villa and in World War I. Little George's father, John, was a U.S. Army sergeant in Cuba during the Spanish-American War. So the lad was greatly affected by his family's military culture.

It is appropriate that his namesakes Uncle George, a respected soldier, and great-great-great-grandfather George, a fabled hunter and founder of the Plott breed, both exemplified what Little George Plott would eventually be—a great hunter and an even greater soldier.

The Plott family was renowned for their hunting ability and for their famous hunting dogs. But they were also good farmers well known for their animal husbandry skills. They were noted for their sheep, cattle and fine horses. Even as a very young boy of only eight years old, Little George began to demonstrate his capability in all these areas, as well as in his schoolwork.

In a charming letter written in careful cursive script to his sister Grace, dated November 8, 1920, Little George wrote in part: "We now have eleven pigs besides the two that run out. Our colt is growing I can lead him where ever I like. I have to go feed the old sow and the horses soon, so I will tell you about my school. I am getting along very well and I am learning fast. I am getting in the third grade as soon as I get my second down." The child concluded his letter with a drawing of the sow and her baby pigs, signing his art work, "George E. Plott drew this."

In addition to their farming and hunting expertise, the Plott men were often known for their volatile tempers and for holding grudges—even among family members. They demanded respect and considered any real or perceived affront to be an insult to their honor. Brothers Von and John Plott, for example, were neighbors and hunted together yet did not speak directly to each other for years over some undisclosed difference.

My Uncle Cecil Plott, an expert bear hunter and horseman from Bryson City, North Carolina, once described the disposition of Plott men this way: "You will never find a better friend or a worse enemy than a Plott. You will respect us for what we do FOR you as our friends, or else for what we will do TO you if you don't respect us. And we never forgive, forget or tolerate insults from anyone—even family."

Little George Plott seemed to somehow be able to bridge all these gaps and work through the family differences. His uncles, George and Von, considered him a son, and his sister Grace and all of his family adored the lad and it is easy to see why they did. He had a bright and positive outlook on life, as evidenced by a poem he wrote at Christmas in 1920:

> *I'm just a tiny little boy,*
> *But in this world of strife,*
> *I'd like to be a Christmas tree*
> *And glitter all my life.*

Little George

Grace and Little George Plott, circa 1914. *Plott Family Collection.*

While the child was clearly a sensitive and articulate boy, he soon became an equally hard-nosed hunter without peer. By the time he was a teenager, Little George Plott was the equal or superior to any hunters in the Great Smoky Mountains. Considering that his Uncle Von Plott is widely considered to be the toughest hunter of his era, the boy had some high standards to adhere to. But he did.

For almost fifteen years—between 1927 and 1941—Little George Plott hunted with the region's best sportsmen on some of the most famous hunts in Great Smoky Mountain hunting history. And he more than held his own with these seasoned nimrods. In 1930, when he was eighteen years old, Little George first became friends with another young hunter named James Oliver Laws. For more than a decade, they shared many hunting adventures together. In 1985, when he was about seventy-five years old, Laws provided some firsthand insight on Little George Plott in a candid interview.

Little George Plott and dogs, circa 1926. *Plott Family Collection.*

The Laws family were well-respected hunters who lived near the head of Hazel Creek, in Swain County, North Carolina. James's father, Jim Laws, killed over one hundred bears in his hunting career and worked as a guide and private game warden for the Hazel Creek Hunting Club. The club members owned more than fifty thousand acres of prime hunting land, most of which is now either under Fontana Lake or part of the Great Smoky Mountains National Park.

James Laws was also employed by the hunting club, and it was where he first met Little George Plott. Laws recalled that the Plott family often drove seventy-five miles from Plott Creek to Hazel Creek on twisting gravel roads to hunt and to breed their dogs with other favored local hounds. Laws added:

> *I liked Little George the best of them all. He was a real sport. Von may have been a better hunter, but he was a lot older and Little George wasn't far behind him even then. Branch Rickey, the famous baseball man was a*

Little George

Little George Plott, left, with Taylor and Kay Wilson. *Plott Family Collection.*

member of the club, and he said that me, Von, and Little George were the mountain runningest hunters he had ever seen.

Laws further elaborated: "Me and my daddy and the Plotts were on ALL the bear hunts up there; we didn't miss any. And we all knew everything they was to know about bears. We knew the day before, what a bear was going to do that night!"

Laws conveys many more interesting stories about Little George and his dogs in the interview, but most of them revolve around specific dogs, such as

Left to right: Little George Plott, Oliver Laws and Taylor Wilson. *Plott Family Collection.*

George's favorite buckskin strike dog or his pure black Plott hound known as Fleet. But one story in particular personifies not only the type of hunter that he was but, more importantly, the caliber of *man* that Little George Plott was.

Baseball manager Branch Rickey, along with several oil executives and Senator William Smathers, was hunting at the Hazel Creek Club in 1935. Little George, James Laws, Wince Cable, Bill Wiggins and Taylor Wilson were serving as their guides. All five guides were later arrested for killing a bear inside the newly formed Great Smoky Mountains National Park. Laws described what happened:

> *Little George and me turned our dogs loose above Granville Calhoun's old place, called the Little Orchard. Some bears was eating apples there and the race was on. Soon it started raining hard and we couldn't hear a thing, not even the barking of our dogs. We huddled up under a big hemlock tree for about four hours to stay dry and wait the storm out. About 2 PM most of the party, except me, Little George, Taylor and my brother-in-laws Wince Cable and Bill Wiggins, wanted to call it a day. But we decided to go look for our dogs. We thought that they probably had a bear treed—and they did.*

Little George

The only problem was that the bear was inside the Great Smoky Mountains National Park, and a federal ranger and state game warden were both waiting for the hunters at the park boundary line. The officials allowed the five men to go into the park *without* their guns to get their dogs and then followed the mountaineers to the bear tree.

Upon their arrival, the bear came down the tree and a vicious bear fight ensued. Laws stated that there were no fewer than seventeen dogs swarming the bear, including the legendary Plott's Scott and one of Von Plott's favorite Airedales. (Von did not breed Airedales to Plott dogs, but he kept several Airedales because he admired their fighting spirit.)

The bear killed a couple of dogs, one of them an Airedale, and went up another tree. The men could not contain all of the dogs as the bruin came back down for another round of fighting. The park ranger supposedly told the hunters that they could kill the bear, but they had no guns and no time to go back and get them. The men had to act fast or else risk losing more dogs to serious injury or death. Little George Plott and James Laws quickly cut a stout sapling and waded into the battle, attempting to pin the beast down, as Taylor Wilson tried to kill it with a knife. Cable and Wiggins, meanwhile, tried to contain the fifteen surviving dogs.

Plott and Laws finally secured the bear with the log and Wilson successfully killed it. The ranger again gave them permission to take the animal out. They carried it almost three miles back to their truck. The hunters then took the bear back to the Hazel Creek Clubhouse and had bear steaks for supper.

The next day, the park superintendent arrived with warrants for the arrests of Plott, Wilson, Cable, Wiggins and Laws. The hunters protested that the charge was unfair, but they were nevertheless arrested and taken thirty-two miles back to Bryson City for arraignment. When they got to the courthouse, the ranger refused to allow them to post bond, but club members Reggie Enloe and Cole Cannon paid their $500 bail. The men were released and a court date for their trial was scheduled.

Little George and friends arrived in Bryson City for their trial, only to find that their case was not on the court docket. The solicitor advised the men to go home and forget about it. Little George Plott would have none of that. He was adamant that he wanted his name cleared and that he wanted the trial over with. Branch Rickey was there supporting Plott and his friends.

Judge Ike Webster agreed that Little George and his party deserved to have their names cleared, and he immediately scheduled their case for that same day. Park officials testified that they had not given permission for the

Von Plott and Plott hounds with an Airedale. *Plott Family Collection*.

Little George

bear kill. They wanted the men prosecuted to the fullest extent of the law. Little George countered that they were only there protecting their dogs. Furthermore, they were doing so with the specific permission of the park officials who were observing them.

Webster wasted no time in handing down his ruling. He agreed that the men had killed the bear for the sake of their dogs and with permission of the rangers. However, he felt that they still should pay a small token fine because he did not want to encourage other hunters to enter the park. Webster asked the hunters if they could afford a five-dollar fine. Little George and his friends happily paid the fee, and their names were cleared. Reggie Enloe reimbursed the men outside the courthouse as they celebrated their victory.

Other locals gathered around and said that they would gladly pay a five-dollar fine to hunt in the park. Plott and Laws quickly dispelled that notion by pointing out that clearing their names and maintaining their honor was what was important to them. They had no desire to poach or hunt bear illegally. Moreover, with their extensive hunting skills and superb dogs, they had no need to.

Von Plott revealed another story about Little George to the Foxfire staff in 1976. It was yet another hunt on Hazel Creek involving Airedales and crossing park boundaries, but this time there were no arrests:

> *Several of us were hunting one time on Hazel Creek in 1937. I had three dogs killed in one fight there. They were all female and my last Airedale was killed in that fight. We had killed one bear already and the dogs split up and some of them turned on another big bear. The park ranger was with me that day; he was watching me, afraid I was going to get on the park land. He stayed with me all day.*
>
> *The sun was nearly gone when we started out after the big bear and I heard a dog. We listened and it [the bear] was running around the side of the mountain and I knew where it was going to cross. I broke and ran up the creek, and saw about three of the dogs.*
>
> *John's boy, Little George was already there, and he said, we had some bad luck ain't we? I said, I don't know George, you tell me. I heard them dogs come through and on toward Bone Valley and I tried to cut them off, but I couldn't.*
>
> *George said, I put them on the bear and the dogs got it treed in the park. But then the ranger told him to go up there and get the dogs away from the tree. But he wouldn't allow us to take any guns on park land.*

Little George

We went up there and looked around and saw that the bear was not but about ten feet off the ground. But then the bear fell out. And it was a big one! The way the dogs latched on you knew that they'd all killed a bear before. The bear didn't do nothing but kill three of them right there—killed two brindle bitches and my last Airedale, a female named Hazel.

Then the bear turned on Little George and run him up a tree. Back then we kept hobnails in our boots, and George ran right up a little maple, got to the top, as high as he could go, and stood up.

That bear went right up that great big sapling and got ahold of the limb that George was on, and George just stomped the hell out of him with his boot! With them old hobnails! I jerked the bear down by its tail and it took off.

George said that the bear had a scar from the left corner of his eye plumb down to his mouth and he had another scar through his chest there as big as a pen. He must have been shot there once; no hair on it. Right down through his chest. George said I'll know him if I ever see him again and I'll kill him.

Two years later, in 1939, Little George Plott played a part in making good his promise. He was hunting with his uncles Von and Big George Plott, his cousin Jim Plott and Reggie Enloe, Ralph Campbell and Joe Parris when their Plott dogs struck a bear trail. The party treed the bear just west of Eagle's Nest Mountain above Plott Valley, where it was killed by Joe Parris. The massive bruin weighed 487 pounds and was easily identifiable by his distinctive scars. A local newspaper carried a story about the hunt and a photo of the bear.

John Plott told a magazine writer a different version of this story in 1949. According to John, his son was only fifteen when he was training four Plott pups and they surprised a big bear. Little George playfully threw a snowball at the bear, thinking that it would run away with his dogs nearby. Instead, the bruin charged him and ran the boy up a sapling. Little George could see the scars on the bear's face as it surged toward him. He was determined to go down fighting as he kicked at the enraged animal. However, his four pups came to his rescue. They attacked the bear and saved Little George's life.

John concluded that the bear retreated after the dogs counterattacked, but not before killing two of the pups. On a hunt later that year, Little George allegedly killed the bear and identified it as the same one that had previously attacked him and killed his dogs.

While an exciting hunting yarn, John's account probably is not true. Newspaper and numerous eyewitness accounts verify Von Plott's version.

A 1935 Branch Rickey hunt near Hazel Creek, North Carolina. Branch Rickey is third from right, Von Plott is second from right and Oliver Laws is at the far right. *Plott Family Collection.*

Furthermore, the dates do not match up, as Little George was fifteen in 1927. The bear in the newspaper story was killed in 1939, when Little George was twenty-seven years old—and George is quoted in the article as identifying the bear as the one he saw on Hazel Creek in 1937.

From 1930 until 1941, Little George Plott would have countless hunting adventures across the mountains of western North Carolina. But it was the 1935 Branch Rickey Hunt, when he was only twenty-three years old, that Little George is probably best known for. James Oliver Laws, Von Plott and Little George Plott were also on the famous October 20, 1935 Branch Rickey Bear Hunt. Though Rickey hunted at Hazel Creek several times, this hunt was the most famous for the number of bears killed in one day—six.

Oliver Laws remembered that he, Branch Rickey, Reggie Enloe, Von Plott, Jim Laws and Bob Haynes each killed one bear on that date. James Laws's bruin was the biggest, weighing well over four hundred pounds. Though Little George harvested no bears himself, he nonetheless made a strong impression on Rickey.

Branch Rickey was working as an executive for the St. Louis Cardinals baseball team at that time and would eventually be inducted into the Baseball Hall of Fame for his efforts in signing Jackie Robinson and integrating professional baseball. In a letter to Von Plott dated December 5, 1935, Rickey thanked and praised Von for the hunt. He then added these comments regarding Little George: "Please give my regards to George. He is a fine boy and he ought to make his mark in the world. Indeed I think he will in whatever he undertakes."

Branch Rickey's words would prove prophetic, as Little George Plott was indeed about to make his mark on the world. But first, he had business to take care of at home.

CITIZEN SOLDIER

While employed as a hunting guide from 1930 to 1940, Little George Plott also helped his father manage their huge Plott Creek farm. In addition, he served as a deputy forest warden. In a letter dated October 17, 1930, Plott was notified that he had been accepted for the position by Charles Flory, assistant forester for the Haywood County District. He was well qualified for the job and it provided the youngster with even more opportunities to enjoy the great outdoors and scout for bear sign.

It was also in 1930, when he was eighteen years old, that Plott made a life-changing decision—he joined the local National Guard unit. Having grown up in a military family, the youngster wanted to perpetuate the warrior legacy. He first considered joining the army, but after the allied victory in World War I—the war to end all wars—military budgets had been slashed. And with the nation mired in the Great Depression, recruiting and enlistment for all branches of the armed services were at an all-time low. Life in a downsized peacetime army held no attraction for the adventurous young mountain hunter.

With no wars to fight, the National Guard seemed a good alternative for Plott. He could gain military experience in the well-respected local guard unit commanded by his Uncle Big George Plott. Yet at the same time, Little George could spend most of his life at home doing what he loved best—hunting, farming and raising Plott bear dogs.

Plott excelled at his guard training. For the next decade, he drilled regularly with his unit and advanced among their ranks. The young man seemed to have a knack for military tactics and strategy. He was a natural leader and a crack shot. With almost twenty years of rugged hunting and farming experience, he was in excellent physical condition. Little George Plott had all the tools needed to be a great soldier.

As Little George matured into manhood, his expertise as a farmer and animal breeder matched his reputation as an expert hunter and citizen soldier. John Plott was apparently somewhat reluctant to turn over his operation to his son, though he grudgingly acknowledged his talents.

In an August 27, 1939 letter to her father, Grace Plott admonished John for not giving her brother George more credit for his work. She further encouraged the elder Plott to allow Little George more money to fund his ideas for improving the place. Grace reminded her father that with George's many talents, John was fortunate to have his son still at home assisting him. John evidently took her advice to heart and began to allow Little George more authority in the business.

Meanwhile, when he wasn't working or training, Little George and his dogs hunted the bear woods hard and often. Sometime around 1940, Little George, his Uncle Von and perhaps his father John were bear hunting with another legendary bear-hunting clan, the Wilsons of nearby Yancey County, North Carolina. It was on this hunt that Plott dog history would be made.

The Plott and Wilson families had hunted together for years. Ewart Wilson had previously rejected Johnson City, Tennessee businessman Hack Smithdeal's offer to buy his hunting dogs, but Wilson invited Smithdeal to join him and the Plott men on a bear hunt. It was on this hunt that Smithdeal first met Little George and Von Plott with a truck full of their Plott bear hounds.

The dogs performed magnificently on the hunt, and Smithdeal was immediately smitten with the breed. He later observed in an interview with historian John Jackson that while he was impressed with *all* of the Plott dogs, there was a definite difference in the manner and appearance of Little George's canines versus those of Von's hounds. Smithdeal stated that the younger Plott's dogs were "a fast, closer fighting, quick and agile dog, while Von's dogs were a more houndy, colder nosed variety, more adept at trailing."

Dempsey Vance was an expert hunter who worked for Smithdeal as a dog handler. Vance described the Plott family hounds: "I don't know how it is, but them hounds know what to do no matter how smart and dog-wise the bear is. If it ain't deep-bred instinct, they sure pick up Plott trade secrets mighty fast!"

Hack Smithdeal and Old Heavy, a dog purchased from the Plott family. *Plott Family Collection.*

After a successful hunt in which several bears were harvested, Smithdeal would not be denied in his efforts to purchase the pack of Plott hounds. After some intense negotiations, he purchased all of the dogs that Von and Little George had brought to the hunt. Thus began a long-term relationship between Smithdeal and the Plott family, as well as the Plott hound's first step toward true national recognition.

And now, with World War II looming on the horizon, master woodsman, farmer and citizen soldier Little George Plott was getting ready to step into the national spotlight as well. On September 1, 1939, the German army invaded Poland. Two days later, American allies England and France declared war on Nazi Germany. Most Americans felt that it was only a matter of time before the United States joined its allies in the fight against Hitler. But back in the mountains of North Carolina, Little George Plott was more concerned with getting his crops harvested and his livestock ready for winter. He was also anticipating another exciting season of bear hunting with his dogs in the Great Smoky Mountains. It was an anniversary of sorts for the Plott family, as they had been hunting in the mountains for almost 150 years.

A pack of Plott dogs owned by John and Little George Plott, 1938. *Plott Family Collection.*

Citizen Soldier

However, the life of Little George Plott was about to take a drastic turn. In September 1940, his National Guard unit was ordered into active duty and shipped to Fort Jackson, South Carolina. It was there, on September 16, 1940, that Lieutenant George Plott was officially commissioned as an officer in the United States Army. He was joined by his cousin, Private Herbert Plott Jr. (son of Hub Plott), and his uncle, Major George Plott, among other local members of the unit.

Though he missed the mountains, his farm, his dogs and hunting, Little George adapted well to full-time military service. Indeed, the young man probably felt that this was his opportunity to make his mark in the world, to truly make a difference—and he did.

For the remainder of 1940 and the first part of 1941, Plott continued to train at Fort Jackson. By the spring of 1941, Little George had been sent to Fort Benning, Georgia, for advanced infantry training. In a letter to his father John, dated June 5, 1941, Little George writes of the intense heat, dust and mosquitoes in Georgia. He adds that though the training was hard, he is doing very well. He also instructs his father to make sure that he keeps a few good dogs for breeding stock so he can continue his Plott dog line after he returned home. He adds wistfully that he knows there would still be plenty of bears to hunt after his service has ended.

The letter is also interesting in that it indicates a rift between Little George and his Uncle Von Plott. Little George had previously been able to stay neutral in the disputes between his father and Uncle Von. But in this case, he clearly sides with his father, though the reasons behind the problem are unclear. Little George writes: "Yes, no doubt Uncle Vaughn thinks that he rules the roost now. Well, the best thing to do is to have nothing to do with him or his dogs either. You get burned every time that you do."

In another letter to his father written in July 1941, Little George makes no further mention of the problem and focuses instead on the difficulty of his training. He further states that he feels like he will be in the military for more than a year—and longer if war is officially declared—but he is unsure of his next station. The remainder of the letter is addressed to farming and dog concerns—the condition of their pasture land, their black lambs, horses and cattle, as well as who wants to buy some of his Plott pups.

Shortly after the bombing of Pearl Harbor, war was declared on the Axis powers, and United States military efforts escalated. However, Little George, his cousin Hub and Uncle Big George still managed to get leave for the Christmas holidays—and a chance for a big bear hunt.

Citizen Soldier

Asheville Citizen Times writer Jack Ruffing did a feature story on the hunt in the Sunday, January 4, 1942 edition of the paper. As noted in "The Next Generations," this hunt would prove notable for several reasons. First and foremost, it is the only documented hunt when seven members of the Plott clan hunted together—Little George, Big George, Von, John, Hub Jr., Cody and Homer Plott all participated in the outing. It would prove to be a reunion in more ways than one, as Little George was also reunited with some of his favorite hunting buddies. James Oliver Laws, Wince Cable, Bill Wiggins and Taylor Wilson—all of whom had been arrested with him on Hazel Creek in 1935—were there, along with Ronald Aldridge and Will Wiggins. And best of all, two veteran hunting legends, seventy-three-year-old Jim Laws and seventy-year-old Mark Cathey, were along to educate and entertain the new generation of Smoky Mountain nimrods. Between them, Cathey and Laws had killed more than 150 bears in their storied careers.

The hunters had their base camp at the Hazel Creek Hunting Club. Though limited hunting with special permits would be allowed in the Great Smoky Mountains National Park until 1946, the formation of the park and the upcoming construction of Fontana Dam would soon leave most of the club's hunting land either under water or off limits to hunters. So this was a sad homecoming for many of the participants, as an era was coming to an end.

And finally, the hunt was significant in that three bears—all weighing over three hundred pounds—were killed in less than two days. While it certainly does not beat the record of six bruins harvested in one day on the 1935 Rickey hunt, it is nonetheless an impressive achievement.

It would also prove to be the last bear hunt for Little George Plott—as he was soon to go off to war.

CHRISTMAS EVE 1944

As the action in World War II intensified, so too did the military training of Little George Plott. Over the next two years—from 1942 to 1944—Plott trained across the United States. By late 1942, he had been promoted to captain and was stationed in Fort Carson, Colorado. It was there that he became close friends with another young army captain, Janna L. Randle. Captain Randle was married and had a young son, Jay Randle, who today fondly recalls his "Uncle" Little George Plott: "My first words were 'jeep'—from the rides he gave me around the base in his jeep—I called him my unca Jerge. Evidently the affection was mutual, because my parents told me about this special relationship on many occasions. He used to tell me that he would give me a Plott hound after the war."

While serving at Fort Carson, Plott was contacted by Hack Smithdeal, who asked if Little George would sell the remainder of his hunting dogs to him. Plott was at first reluctant to do so. But after being assured again by his father that he would retain some breeding stock for his son until after the war, he reconsidered the offer. Smithdeal later related to historian John Jackson that Little George said he wanted his dogs to have the opportunity to hunt often. He knew that his hounds missed hunting almost as much as he did, so he took their best interests to heart and sold most of his pack to Smithdeal in 1942.

The 66th Infantry Black Panther Division was activated from various combined National Guard and U.S. Army units at Camp Blanding, Florida, on April 15, 1943. Later that summer, Captain George Plott took command of Company H, 81st Mortar Platoon of the 262nd Regiment of the 66th Infantry Division. Shortly after that, the division moved to Fort Robinson, Arkansas, for advanced training. Little George's letters home during this period indicate a pride in his platoon but also sadness at missing another season of bear hunting with his family, friends and their dogs.

Lieutenant Alex Brown Jr. was a member of Company H and he knew Plott well. He remembers Little George "as a fine officer who was good to his troops. His men were very well-trained with very high morale." Other troops recall that their captain was "firm but fair. It was all very black and white with him. He knew the rules and he followed them to the letter. We nicknamed him Captain 'by the book' Plott."

Captain Little George Plott, 1944. *Plott Family Collection.*

The Sixty-sixth Division arrived at Fort Rucker, Alabama, for six months' of tactical training in April 1944. Perhaps it was a premonition, or maybe it was nothing more than a case of mountain practicality, but on September 21, 1944, Little George Plott wrote his last will and testament. In it he stated that his sister Grace was to be the sole beneficiary of his life insurance policy—a plan on which he paid a thirty-one-dollar premium semiannually. Plott then forwarded the will and other personal papers to his sister for safekeeping.

With their training in Alabama completed, Little George Plott and his division sailed for Europe and arrived at Dorchester, England, in November 1944. As the Battle of the Bulge began on December 16, 1944, the war in Europe had reached a critical tipping point. Reinforcements were desperately needed for the frostbitten American troops surrounded by Germans in the Ardennes Forest.

Christmas Eve 1944

On December 23, 1944, the Sixty-sixth Infantry received their orders to reinforce the troops locked in the frigid Ardennes. At 2:00 p.m. that day, Captain Plott gathered his platoon and told them to saddle up—they were to board the SS *Leopoldville* at midnight to cross the English Channel. They should arrive in Cherbourg, France, by 6:00 p.m. on Christmas Eve. As he dismissed his unit to load their gear, Plott hesitated and called them back to attention. At the last minute, Captain Plott decided that about fifty of his men—all first and second gunners—would fall out and ride in jeeps and trucks aboard open vehicle landing ships, known as LSTs.

Cloyce Gibson was one of these gunners, and he was none too happy about the decision. He was angry that his comrades would sail in relative warmth and comfort while he suffered on the open seas in the damp, frigid air. But the order ultimately saved his life.

As they prepared to board the *Leopoldville*, the other 55 troops of Company H were equally unexcited about spending their Christmas holiday as a target for German submarines. The *Leopoldville* was a former luxury liner named for the capital of the Belgian Congo. It was originally designed to house 361 passengers but had been commissioned by the British navy and re-outfitted in 1939 as a military transport ship capable of holding more than 2,000 troops.

As the 262nd and 264th Regiments of the 66th Division clambered up the gangplank at midnight, they were met by the ship's civilian captain, a war-weary Belgian sailor named Charles Limor. As the Americans boarded the ship, they no doubt assumed that Limor's silent countenance was due to arrogance or fatigue. But the truth was that neither Captain Limor nor his 213-man crew spoke a word of English—only Flemish.

As a result, none of the Americans was given instructions as to how to evacuate the boat, deploy their lifeboats or even how to properly use the kopak life jackets—which if not used correctly would break the necks of their users. To make matters worse, there were only enough life jackets for about half of the passengers.

By 2:00 a.m. on Christmas Eve morning, 2,235 members of the Sixty-sixth Infantry Division were safely aboard the *Leopoldville*. Little George's unit—Company H—slept fitfully in the lowest starboard hold of the ship, well below water level. Captain Plott and his junior officers were in cabins just above them.

Meanwhile, back in the mountains of North Carolina, John Plott had recently gone bear hunting with Ewart Wilson in Yancey County. Their hunt had been a successful one, but Little George was sorely missed. As they gathered around the fire that night, John confided to Wilson and his wife, Essie, that he was concerned for the safety of his son. Like many mountain folk, the elder Plott believed strongly in premonitions. And lately he had experienced ominous feelings about his boy. John asked the Wilsons to pray for both him and his son as he retired for the evening.

More than 3,500 miles away, Christmas Eve dawned clear and cold as the *Leopoldville* pulled out of Southampton, England, at 7:00 a.m. The vessel was escorted in a diamond formation by the HMS *Brilliant* and three additional ships—a Coast Guard cutter, an ATR3 tug and a British minesweeper. The *Leopoldville* practiced evasive zigzag maneuvers, hoping to avoid German subs, as it chugged across the rough waters of the English Channel. The *Brilliant* and some of the other boats that accompanied them dropped depth charges, also known as "little boys," to ward off Nazi U-boats.

The men of Company H took comfort in the dull thumping of the exploding depth charges, thinking that they were well protected. Little did they know that they were being stalked by a German submarine commanded by Captain Gerhard Meyer.

At about 3:30 p.m., the melancholy troops gathered to eat a greasy, gray stew for their holiday dinner. Christmas carols crackled through the speakers of radios and record players as the thoughts of the men drifted back to past holidays more happily spent at home. Captain Plott sent Lieutenant Alex Brown Jr. below deck to check on the men. Plott was likely homesick too, as he reflected on his own family, as well as yet another missed bear-hunting season.

Brown returned to the officers' mess on B Deck at 5:00 p.m. and reported to Plott that the men were fine. But after eating dinner with the other officers, Lieutenant Brown did not feel well himself—he had a terrible toothache. As he went below to check on the men again at 5:45 p.m., Brown took a brief detour back to his cabin to get some aspirin. It was a decision that saved his life.

A few minutes after that, U-boat Captain Meyer fired his first torpedo at the *Leopoldville*—but it missed. Meyer quickly made adjustments and launched a second torpedo. It did not miss. At 5:54 p.m., it exploded into the starboard quarter of the ship—a direct hit on the fifty-five men of Company H who were relaxing below deck.

The explosion caused the ship to lurch badly, but most of the men above were still unaware that they were under attack. They assumed that a boiler had exploded. Instead, 253 men, including almost all of Company H, were killed instantly or injured and trapped below in the blast. Water rushed into the pierced hull and huge, tangled pieces of red-hot metal maimed those still alive and prevented their escape. Ladders or stairs were destroyed or impassable.

At 6:45 p.m., Captain Little George Plott and two of his junior officers—Lieutenant Brown and another lieutenant named Lee—calmly assessed the situation. Brown recalls that Plott was devastated by the loss of his soldiers and commented sadly, "Thank God that I sent the other men with the trucks and jeeps, or else they'd be dead too." But Plott quickly regained his composure and developed an action plan.

In the meantime, the ship's Belgian commander, Captain Limor, stood by and did nothing. He did not even attempt to send out radio distress signals or shoot rescue flares. Plott and Brown realized that they were only five miles off the coast of France and remained confident that the surviving troops would be rescued.

Captain Plott gave orders to tend to the wounded and began to coordinate rescue and evacuation efforts as the HMS *Brilliant* pulled aside the *Leopoldville*. Plott ordered Brown and Lee, among others, to leap aboard the British destroyer. Lee jumped first and made it safely. Brown stated that he intended to stay with his captain until he could escape too. Plott said that he could not go yet but assured Brown that he would follow closely behind him. Little George sternly ordered him to join Lee on the *Brilliant*, and Brown reluctantly did so.

As the *Brilliant* pulled away from the *Leopoldville* at 7:00 p.m., Captain Plott and other officers courageously tried to deploy the lifeboats but were unable to do so. Tragically, there were more than enough boats for all the soldiers, yet the Belgian crew made no effort to help the Americans. By 7:30 p.m., the Belgians (with the exception of Captain Limor) had abandoned the *Leopoldville* and sailed away with their own life rafts less than half full. The Americans were left alone to fend for themselves.

Lawrence Tohey was in Company K of the 262nd and watched as Lee and Brown, along with about five hundred others, jumped to safety onto the HMS *Brilliant*. Tohey later wrote that Captain Plott and a few others had coils of rope and were attempting to rappel below deck to rescue survivors. This was a virtual suicide mission, but further reports indicate that Plott probably made two successful rescue attempts below deck and attempted a third try—perhaps more.

Hundreds of men on deck, including Lawrence Tohey, now realized that help was not coming and that the *Leopoldville* was going to sink. Survivors began to search frantically for life jackets, but there weren't enough to go around. This did not deter Captain Plott, who continued his rescue efforts. Tohey lost sight of Little George after that, as the ship listed to about forty-five degrees. Tohey was one of the few who not only found a life jacket, but also knew how to use it. He plunged into the indigo water and was rescued two hours later by a French tugboat.

It was now 7:40 p.m., and there are conflicting stories as to the status of Little George Plott. As the ship rolled over and began to sink, Plott almost certainly was still below deck on at least his third rescue attempt. He was presumably trapped there. Alex Brown Jr. was told by another survivor that he later saw Plott in the water still alive. Though possible, this is highly unlikely based on the three other reports.

Lieutenant S.J. Lewandowski, commander of U.S. Navy ATR-3 salvage tug, recoiled in horror as he arrived on the scene at 7:45 p.m. He had seen a distress signal from the *Brilliant*, but he did not fully realize the severity of the situation. The lieutenant switched on his powerful twenty-four-inch spotlights and scanned the darkness looking for survivors.

The dull moonlight combined with the harsh glare of the electrical lamps to create contrasting eerie shadows on the dead and dying. A few survivors clung to the rapidly sinking *Leopoldville*, shouting for help. Others bobbed glassy eyed in the frigid water suffering from shock, hypothermia or other injuries. Many lay face down in the turbulent seas, dead from drowning or broken necks. Body parts and debris floated around them. A constant moan permeated the salty air, interrupted frequently by screams, curses and more often the sound of men praying.

Lewandowski radioed or signaled for help. For the next fifty-five minutes, Lieutenant Lewandowski's tug, along with several other military and private vessels who had responded to his call, focused on rescuing survivors. The HMS *Brilliant* made no effort to return to aid them or even radio for assistance, nor was any help dispatched from ports in either England or France. The men of the Sixty-sixth Infantry Division had for the most part been betrayed by their allies as well as their own military.

The night skies were suddenly illuminated by flames at 8:40 p.m. as the boilers of the *Leopoldville* exploded. If there were any survivors still below deck then, the blasts killed them. The ship sunk deeper into the English Channel, now on its end with only the tip of the bow above water. By 8:54 p.m.—a little over two hours after being attacked—the *Leopoldville* finally sank. The suction and turbulence of the water as the ship submerged drowned many of the remaining survivors still in the ocean.

Lewandowski and a few other brave ship captains continued their rescue efforts until well after midnight. They saved over 1,600 men and returned to port on Christmas morning with their decks littered with 264 corpses.

Christmas Eve 1944

John Plott and his second wife, Nora, 1936. *Plott Family Collection.*

Of the 2,235 American troops aboard the *Leopoldville*, 802 died on Christmas Eve 1944. Soldiers from forty-seven of the then existing forty-eight states died in the tragedy, including three sets of brothers and two sets of twins. Captain Little George Plott was among the dead. Yet the British and American governments chose for years to ignore this tragedy. With the Battle of the Bulge still in question, they wanted nothing to detract from the Allied war efforts, nor did they want to acknowledge how they had failed the Sixty-sixth Infantry Division. Instead, they declared the men missing or killed in action and kept all facts about the incident classified until 1959.

John Plott died in 1959 without knowing the details of his son's tragic demise. The old man never fully recovered from the death of his only boy. He kept Little George's room just as he had left it in 1940 until his own passing almost twenty years later. And to honor him, John Plott continued to breed Plott hunting dogs for the remainder of his life.

Grace Plott refused to acknowledge the death of her brother for years. She continued to pay his insurance premiums in hopes that he would one day return. In a 1945 letter to his insurance company, Grace wrote: "I refuse to accept this as final, but rather to admit a period of anxiety after which he will return." She lived to learn of the coverup and remained bitter about it until her death.

Homeplace of Little George Plott today. *Courtesy of John Jackson.*

The body of Captain Little George Plott was never found. We cannot say for sure exactly what killed him. But thanks to the reports from *Leopoldville* survivors Lawrence Tohey, Carson Kirk, Alex Brown Jr. and Kenneth Kline, we do know for certain that he died a hero.

Carson Kirk described it best, as he wrote bittersweetly in 1993: "There can be no doubt that Captain Plott stayed behind to rescue his men. He was one of many heroes of the 66th Infantry Division who gave their lives trying to save others on that awful night. He was the kind of person who should be honored on our postage stamps. But don't hold your breath because it will never happen."

Little George Plott was the veteran of numerous challenging and dangerous hunting trips. As a child in 1920, Plott had written sweetly of aspiring to brighten a world filled with strife. Those aspirations came true on Christmas Eve 1944 as the thirty-two-year-old mountaineer saved his most valiant effort for his last hunt—a manhunt in which he searched for and attempted to rescue his men.

The New Testament Book of John 15:13 reads: "Greater love hath no man than this, that a man lay down his life for his friends." That brief Bible verse would have been the perfect epitaph for Captain George Plott. There were many mountain hunters who hunted longer than Little George Plott and perhaps a few who were as good as or superior to him. But *none* was a better man.

"A WOODS ROVING FAMILY"

The Rich family first came to Haywood County in the early 1870s, about seventy-five years after the Plotts. The Rich clan settled a few miles northwest of Robert Henry Plott in a rugged, remote cove that would soon be named after them—Rich Cove.

Though they were late to arrive to Maggie Valley, the Rich family quickly established themselves as one of the premier hunting clans in the Great Smoky Mountains. The Riches were members of an elite group of pioneer settlers that was totally self-sufficient. They not only lived entirely off the land, but they also lived relatively well in the process. In 1952, feature writer Harold Martin accurately described the Rich clan as being "a woods roving family, fond of the taste of wild game." And today, almost 150 years later, some members of the Rich family still possess those same capabilities.

Tom Alexander, a noted woodsman, businessman and former United States Forest Service ranger, was founder of the Cataloochee Ranch and ski resort. It was one of the earliest high-quality tourist destinations in the Great Smokies and remains so today. Alexander hired many local folks to work there, and they respected him greatly as an employer and, more importantly, as a friend.

One of the many families that Alexander hired and befriended when he first arrived to the region in the 1930s was the Rich family. In his book *Mountain Fever* (edited by Tom Alexander Jr. and Jane Alexander), Alexander described the Rich clan this way:

> *Several times a year we might see the men from the Rich family, who lived in a neighboring cove, heading across our field for the woods with rifles on their shoulders and a dog or two in tow. Their sole camping gear would consist of hunting jackets whose pockets might contain a length of fishing line and some hooks, a chunk or two of corn bread and perhaps a little ground meal, salt, and ground coffee. Thus equipped they would remain in the wilds for days, rain or shine, sleeping on the bare ground under an overhanging rock or between two big fires, subsisting largely on what they killed, caught, picked, or dug up—squirrels, groundhogs, trout, grouse, nuts, berries, wild leeks and so forth.*
>
> *Mostly their armament would consist of .22 caliber rifles or single-shot shotguns, but sometimes one of the older men would be seen carrying an ancient muzzle-loading rifle, the long graceful type of weapon used by Daniel Boone and the frontier fighters of the American Revolution.*

Were it not for Tom Alexander's brief mention of them in his book, as well as the 1952 *Saturday Evening Post* article, the Rich family would have remained in relative obscurity in Smoky Mountain hunting history. But they were equal or superior to many mountain hunters—they just weren't as well known.

Sabert Rich

The Smoky Mountain hunting saga of the Rich family began with Sabert Rich's birth in Powell's Valley, Tennessee, in 1854. It was an area not unlike the Great Smokies, with abundant fishing and hunting, and it proved to be a good place for young Sabert to hone his woodcraft. But the Civil War changed all that.

The Riches, like many southern families, found their house divided when the war began. Some of the Rich clan sided with the Union while others fought for the Confederacy, resulting in wounds that not even time could heal. Sabert was too young to fight in the conflict, but reportedly his father and some of his brothers supported and fought for the South. As a result, they were persecuted and ostracized by their Federal family sympathizers and neighbors after the war.

When Sabert was nearly twenty years old, he decided to leave home. He debated on heading out west, but a malaria outbreak in Arkansas forced him

Sabert Rich. *Courtesy of Steven and Linda Rich.*

instead to return back east, first to Tennessee and soon after that, in 1874, to Haywood County, North Carolina.

Sabert, a skilled hunter, found the Great Smoky Mountains to his liking. The area provided him with everything he needed—food, water and solace and refuge from the war. He located his homesite on a high, south-facing ridge supported by a cold, bold spring and enough flat land for a decent garden. His initial claim was for about sixty acres of land. Tax receipts show the tax value on the property as being less than three dollars.

Rich built a cabin here, in the area now known as Rich Cove, and made his living mostly as a hunter, trapper, farmer and logger. In 1875, Sabert married Catherine "Tine" Finger, a member of another notable local hunting family. Together they would raise eight children and eventually acquire almost one thousand acres of land reaching from Evans Cove to Fie Branch to the top of Buck Mountain—the site of the present-day tourist attraction Ghost Town.

Tine Finger was not only a devoted mother and housewife, but she was an esteemed midwife in the community as well. She delivered hundreds of mountain children. Tine helped deliver her last child when she was seventy-five years old.

Sabert and Tine's first son—John Calvin Rich, born in 1876—inherited his mother's love for the field of medicine. He later became a doctor in Haywood and Buncombe Counties. Dr. John Rich is believed to have delivered more than three thousand children in his thirty-six-year medical career. More significantly, he is remembered fondly as a doctor who *never* refused to visit a sick person in need.

Their other four boys—William Amos, born in 1878; Charles Thomas, born in 1880; David Franklin, born in 1885; and James Clauson, born in 1892—took after their father Sabert. They hit the woods running hard and they never turned back.

James Clauson Rich

According to his descendants, James "Jim" Rich was very frugal. In later life, he moved to nearby Evans Cove, but Jim developed his woodsman skills and thrifty manner while growing up in Rich Cove.

His prudent nature got the best of him in the 1940s while he was squirrel hunting near his home. It was an unseasonably hot September day when

"A Woods Roving Family"

Jim came upon the biggest bear that he had ever seen. It was well over five hundred pounds, and he could not resist shooting it. Rich was elated that the kill could provide him with enough meat for months. But he soon realized that the beast was far too big for him to field dress alone, much less transport back home. So Jim left the carcass and later convinced several of his friends to help him field dress the bruin and carry it out.

Rich's buddies agreed to help, but did so thinking that he would divide the bear meat with them, as old-time hunters traditionally did. Smoky Mountain bear hunters usually followed a simple but fair system to ensure that everyone in the hunting party got meat for his efforts.

Whoever shot or actually killed the bear got the rights to the bear hide. Then, after the bear was skinned and field dressed, one person butchered and separated the bear meat into shares. The idea was to keep the shares as equal as possible and to include some choice cuts of meat in each amount. Then another hunter would shut his eyes and turn his back to the meat. The butcher would point at each pile of meat and call out loudly, "Whose meat is this?" The fellow with his eyes closed would respond by naming a hunter in the party, who would later come forward to claim his share. This process continued until every member of the group received his cut. Hunters weren't always happy with the outcome—especially in larger groups—but they respected the system and usually adhered to it without much complaint.

When his friends explained to Jim Rich that they expected to be compensated in the traditional manner for their efforts, Rich flatly refused. Jim argued that they had no part in the actual hunt or kill, and as a result they were owed nothing. His companions responded that they deserved at least a share of the meat for their assistance in butchering the massive animal and hauling it out.

A heated argument resulted in a standoff—Rich would not share his bear, and his friends refused to help him if he didn't. After a while, they returned angrily to their homes as Jim stubbornly tried to skin the bruin and salvage the meat for himself. But the sheer bulk of the beast prevented him from doing so. He could not even drag the carcass to a creek to cool and preserve it. It did not take long before the meat spoiled in the late summer heat. This was one instance in which Rich's tightfisted nature bordered on being stubbornly greedy, and it resulted in the loss of a bountiful harvest of bear meat.

However, other aspects of his self-sufficiency were admirable and were qualities shared by the entire Rich clan, then and now. These mountaineers wasted nothing. They particularly relished groundhog hunting and put every part of the animal to good use. In addition to enjoying the savory meat, they made shoestrings and banjo heads from the hides and cough medicine from the grease. The family would render the fat from a groundhog (or a bear) into grease and mix it with sulfur or honey to produce an effective remedy for chest colds.

While the Rich family today can still laugh about Jim Rich not sharing his hunting bounty, they nevertheless appreciate and admire his strong-willed sense of independence. Moreover, they admire his tenacity in adhering to old-time traditions. These were qualities shared by all the Rich brothers, including the ageless muzzleloading champions Amos and Charlie Rich.

WILLIAM AMOS RICH AND CHARLES THOMAS RICH

Little information is available regarding William Amos Rich and Charles Thomas Rich. A few facts, however, are clear. They were both crack shots and they both participated and did well in the earliest muzzleloading rifle competitions held at the Cataloochee Ranch.

After hay season ended in about 1945, Cataloochee Ranch owner Tom Alexander decided that his friends and employees deserved a reward for their

Charles Rich competing at the Cataloochee Beef Shoot. *Cataloochee Ranch Collection.*

"A Woods Roving Family"

Shooting match at the Cataloochee Ranch. *Cataloochee Ranch Collection.*

hard work. So began the first annual Cataloochee Beef Shoot—a contest similar to shooting matches first held on the early American frontier.

The rules were simple. Participants were separated into four age groups: nineteen and under, twenty to thirty-nine, forty to sixty and those over sixty

Left to right: Amos Rich, Tom Alexander and Charlie Rich. *Cataloochee Ranch Collection.*

years of age. Shooters were allowed to use only primitive muzzleloading black powder rifles and were allowed three shots at their respective targets. Each target had three cross marks on it. The idea was to either directly hit the cross mark or as close to it as possible. Judges determined the winner by measuring the distance of each shot from the cross mark. The shooter with the lowest three-shot total measurement won the match.

Shooters paid one dollar to compete for prime beef prizes. Steer were quartered, and the forequarters were awarded to the two youngest age class winners and the hindquarters to the victors from the two older age groups. The best overall shot took home the steer hide and beef tallow. The Cataloochee Shoot started out as a small neighborly contest, but before it ended in the late 1960s, more than one hundred shooters regularly participated in the annual event.

Legend has it that Charlie and Amos Rich—both nearly seventy years old—placed first and second in their elderly age group at these earliest competitions. No one knows for sure who won, but they both continued to compete strongly in the shoots until shortly before their deaths. A photo of the Rich brothers with Tom Alexander shows them with their rifles, wearing overalls, slouch hats and long, snow white beards. They were the epitome of the early mountain hunter. Though the picture was taken in the mid-1940s, it just as easily could have been the 1840s.

Charlie Rich's oldest son, Columbus "Punk" Rich, was a master gunsmith. A .32-caliber muzzleloading rifle that Punk built was a treasured Rich family heirloom, as was a .22-caliber single-shot breakdown pistol patterned after a modern H&R model. Punk's uncle, David Franklin Rich, would eventually own these weapons. And he would put them to good use, as would his son, Floyd Rich.

David Franklin Rich

David Franklin "Frank" Rich, affectionately known as "Poppy," was the fourth son of Sabert and Tine Rich. He was born in 1885. Frank and his son, Robert Floyd Rich, were undoubtedly the two best hunters, trappers and possibly marksmen in the Rich clan. Indeed, a good argument could be made that Frank and Floyd Rich were two of the all-time best hunters in Smoky Mountain hunting history.

This dynamic father-son duo hunted and trapped in the Great Smoky Mountains for a combined total of more than one hundred years, and they *each* killed more than one hundred bears in the course of their storied careers. The Rich boys also made some of the finest white liquor ever produced in these mountains.

While in his late teens, Frank Rich built a two-story frame house in Rich Cove. Shortly after that, in 1907, he married into another renowned hunting and moonshining family—the Sutton clan. The union of Frank Rich and Annie Mae Sutton produced four children, three of whom were boys. All became excellent outdoorsmen, but none better than their youngest son, Robert Floyd, who was born in 1916.

Like his father before him, Frank supported his growing family by hunting, trapping, logging and farming. When he wasn't tending his own farm, Frank would go over the mountain to the settlement of Cataloochee and help friends or relatives there stack hay, put up tobacco and round up hogs to kill.

In those days, fences were mostly used to keep livestock *out* of gardens and fields—not retain them. Farmers marked their cows and swine and then released them to range the surrounding peaks to forage for grass on the mountain balds and chestnuts and mast in the thick forest.

Above: Frank Rich homeplace. *Courtesy of Steven and Linda Rich.*

Below: Herding hogs across the gap. *Courtesy of Great Smoky Mountains National Park Archives.*

Cattle would be branded for identification, while hogs received a distinctive notch on one or both ears indicating their owner. They would then be released in the spring and checked on several times during the summer before being rounded up again in the late fall.

"A Woods Roving Family"

Often, farmers would attach a bell collar to a lead hog that they released. The other pigs would usually stay close to the leader, and the bell made him easier to locate. But it also required maintenance, as the farmer/hunters had to return occasionally to loosen the collar on the lead boar as it fattened up on mast.

Mountaineers often combined business with pleasure, as they usually fished and hunted on these livestock-ranging trips. Frank Rich brought his hunting dogs with him to help locate his farm animals as well as to hunt squirrels, groundhogs, turkeys, grouse and raccoons. The Rich family favored blue tick and redbone dogs for their small game hunting and Plott hounds for bear, wild boar and sometimes raccoons.

Frank Rich loading his muzzleloading rifle. *Courtesy of Steven and Linda Rich.*

LEGENDARY HUNTERS OF THE SOUTHERN HIGHLANDS

George Alexander, right, with one of the judges at the Cataloochee Ranch shooting match. *Cataloochee Ranch Collection.*

"A Woods Roving Family"

While on one of these trips, Frank Rich is said to have killed what was then the last turkey in the Great Smokies. The turkey population has thankfully since made a comeback, but by the early 1940s, men like Rich and "Turkey" George Palmer had about wiped them out. Rich was hunting on the Ledge Bald, near Beech Gap in the Plott Balsam Range, when he first heard the gobbler. Frank hid in the thicket and called it in using only a laurel leaf and a forked twig to duplicate the turkey call. The bird slowly approached him, and he shot its head off with his .32-caliber muzzleloading rifle. This was one of the two guns built for Frank by Punk Rich. Frank later passed both weapons down to his son Floyd.

Once the livestock was located and contained, the hunting fun was over and the real work began. The animals were then driven back to their respective farms. Upon returning home, the animals were fed corn for a few weeks to further fatten them up. They were then slaughtered and butchered. Hog killing was a bloody but highly anticipated and festive occasion. Neighbors gathered to help one another in the process and usually dined on fresh pork tenderloin and sausage. It was often like a big Thanksgiving feast with music, plenty of food and thanks for a good harvest.

The Cataloochee Beef Shoots were usually held around harvest time too. Like his older brothers, Frank Rich excelled at these competitions. Rich was at least sixty years old when the contests began, but it is believed that he entered the forty- to sixty-year-old category so as not to compete with Amos and Charlie. He usually won the matches or finished in the top five. Later, when his older brothers no longer competed, Frank dominated the over-sixty age group and participated in the events until he was over seventy-five years old.

Using the same .32-caliber rifle that he competed with, Frank Rich wreaked havoc on the local bear population—killing or trapping more than one hundred bruins. Only the most accurate marksmen can use such a small-bore gun to bring down big game. The shot has to be perfectly placed to kill a bear. And accuracy was even more critical using a single-shot muzzleloader. With no time to reload, one round *had* to be a kill shot unless you were prepared to face a raging bruin in hand-to-hand combat. But Frank Rich made his shots count each and every time.

Fur trapping was another method employed by many mountain hunters to make money. There were few better at it than Frank Rich. He trapped all sizes of game, from bears to skunks, but the market for hides predominantly dealt in small game. A flyer sent to the Rich home in 1938 from the New York firm of David Blustein and Brothers lists the following prices per prime pelt:

Otter: Twelve dollars.
Prime Mink: Five to seven dollars.
Red Fox: Three dollars.
Raccoon: Two dollar and fifty cents.
Grey Fox: One dollar and seventy-five cents.
Skunk: Eighty-five cents.
Muskrat: Seventy to ninety cents.
Weasel: Sixty cents.
Possum: Sixty cents.

Family members recall that Frank Rich regularly brought in hundreds of pounds of pelts every year. Hides were obtained by hunting, too, particularly in the case of raccoons. And again, this is where the Rich family hunting dogs played an integral role in their success.

Resourceful trappers maximized their time in the woods by hunting while checking their trap lines or by looking for wild ginseng. Frank regularly found and harvested patches of the wild plant while roaming the hills. Dried ginseng roots sold for about $7 to $8 a pound in the 1930s and '40s. That same amount today would sell for $900 or more per pound. Obviously it took a lot of pelts and wild ginseng to make even a few dollars in those days. But a few dollars went a long way in the Depression era—especially in the mountains. However, that often still wasn't enough.

Frank further supplemented his income by making liquor. We don't know for sure if he learned his craft from his in-laws, the Suttons, or if someone from within the Rich family taught him. But Frank Rich believed in using only the best quality materials in the production of his stills, as well as in the making of his liquor.

Rich felt that it was his God-given right to make liquor, and he felt that he was doing nothing wrong. Liquor making was simply a way to help support his family. Since he paid taxes on the sugar and copper that he bought, and grew his own corn, as well as did the labor himself, what was wrong with making liquor?

The federal government certainly found plenty wrong with it, but it was never able to catch him. Frank taught the art of hunting, trapping *and* liquor making to his son Floyd, who carried on the family tradition deep into the twentieth century.

"A Woods Roving Family"

ROBERT FLOYD RICH

By the time Floyd Rich was seventeen in 1933, he had made more liquor and killed more bears than most men twice his age. As soon as the lad could walk, his father had the boy in the woods teaching him wilderness survival skills. Tracking, hunting, trapping, fishing, reading animal signs, predicting the weather, identifying edible and medicinal plants and mastering all forms of firearms became second nature to the youngster. The lad could field dress and skin a bear quicker and cleaner than anyone in the mountains.

As he matured, liquor making was added to the lesson plan. Young Floyd was quick to master that as well. Floyd wasn't a big man—he stood only about five feet, five inches tall—but he was incredibly strong and possessed the constitution of a workhorse. Rich routinely placed a one-hundred-pound sack of sugar over each shoulder and carried the load for miles without stopping to some of the most remote liquor still sites in the mountains.

The Rich family with a sample of their moonshine in a jar. Floyd Rich is top left. *Courtesy of Steven and Linda Rich.*

Once the liquor was distilled, it was poured into gallon jars, sealed, placed in a burlap tow sack and transported back to town to sell. Each of these jars weighed about ten pounds, and a sack could hold eight to ten jars. It is said that Floyd could carry two sacks of liquor back down to Maggie Valley without rest, and without breaking a jar.

The heavy workload eventually took a toll on his body. On a return trip down a steep slope in the late 1930s, a bone in his right leg literally snapped due to the stress. Fortunately, no liquor was lost, and Rich quickly recovered.

Floyd knew the location of every cold water spring in the region and, like his father, believed in making high-quality moonshine. He had stills scattered all over Haywood County, including several in Rich Cove. Frequent hunting and fishing trips with his family and other elite local nimrods such as members of the Frady, Sutton, McGha, Mehaffey, Messer and Plott clans provided Rich with ample opportunity to target potential new still sites. Floyd hunted, trapped or fished almost daily year-round.

While hunting in Graham County, North Carolina, Rich scouted out additional prime spots for stills and made liquor there. Though he lived in Rich Cove his entire life, Floyd loved the rugged mountains of Graham or neighboring Swain County. Some of the best hunting and fishing in the Great Smoky Mountains could be found here, as well as some of the greatest hunters who ever lived—and Floyd Rich knew them all. Rich hunted with such sporting icons as Mark Cathey, Granville Calhoun, Cotton McGuire, Sam Hunnicutt and Dewey Sharp, along with various members of the Denton, Hooper and Orr clans. Dewey Sharp would later remember Floyd Rich as being as good as any of them.

To get to his Graham or Swain County hunting grounds, Rich initially walked about twenty miles to Bryson City and caught a train to the small logging community of Proctor, North Carolina. Later in life, he would drive a 1930 Willis Jeep to the area. From there, Rich could hunt the entire Hazel Creek watershed and then roam farther west into the Snowbird and Santeetlah region of Graham County. With only minimal provisions, a bedroll and a gun, Rich would hunt here for weeks at a time.

Though some of these prime sporting areas were acquired by the Great Smoky Mountains National Park in 1934, hunters were allowed permits to hunt the Hazel Creek drainage until 1946. Floyd avidly hunted in the park until he was thirty years old and frequently hunted the other surrounding areas the remainder of his life.

Rich was particularly good friends with the Hooper family and enjoyed hunting on the mountain named for them—Hooper's Bald. The peak was the site of one of the region's most famous hunting lodges, which was established by Whiting Manufacturing in 1912 and later sold to Champion Paper in 1926. Another of Rich's hunting buddies—Cotton McGuire—was the game warden for the lodge and lived on the mountain most of his life. European boars were released at the lodge in 1912. The boars mated with feral hogs and remain a fierce pest to the region still today.

Floyd Rich killed many bears here as well as numerous wild boars. He was so impressed with the area, especially Hooper's Bald, that he would later insist that his first grandson, Tony, be named after the mountain. Tony Hooper Rich, born in 1956, carries on the Rich family hunting legacy today, along with his son Sidney.

Probably because he was so ambitious, with so many liquor stills spread across the region, Floyd was eventually arrested for bootlegging. He got off with a warning and a fine the first time. But he went right back to making homebrew. However, after being apprehended a second time, the judge not only gave him a stiffer fine, but also promised Rich that if he was caught again he would spend a *long* time in prison. The thought of jail time was too much for the free-ranging mountaineer, and Rich never made liquor again.

Instead, he found another dangerous but legal vocation—logging. Rich worked in several rugged logging camps on Fines Creek, near Max Patch,

Floyd Rich, far left, working as a logger. *Courtesy of Steven and Linda Rich.*

and in the region known as Twelve Mile near the Tennessee border. The men worked six days a week for a dollar a day and they were paid by the company with silver dollars. A neighbor, realizing the value of silver, would buy the coins from the loggers with paper money. It all spent the same to the timbermen, and they gladly made the exchange.

Rich was never hurt while cutting logs, but he nearly lost his arm in a truck wreck in the 1940s. He was driving a lumber truck along a narrow road above Fines Creek when his brakes went out and the vehicle overturned, severing his right bicep. Though seriously injured, Rich recovered, and he eventually regained use of his arm. From then on, Floyd devoted his life entirely to farming, hunting, digging ginseng and trapping.

Floyd had married the former Nola Frady in about 1934, and they first set up household in what had originally been an old barn in Rich Cove. Rich insisted that wild game be served in his house three meals a day—and he had no trouble providing it. Bear, groundhog, squirrel, rabbit and grouse, along with various vegetables and hog meat raised on their farm, was standard table fare for the Rich family. Floyd and Nola made sure that no one ever went hungry in their home. Grouse was a favorite delicacy of Floyd's, and he enjoyed it often, both at home as well as in hunting camps. But his method of hunting grouse was unusual and is testament to his tremendous shooting skills.

Due to their incredible speed and near invisibility in the field, grouse are difficult to kill, even with a shotgun. They frequent mountain forests and underbrush, usually in small groups of four to ten birds, and they will eat almost anything. Huge flocks of grouse once lived in the Great Smoky Mountains. By the early 1900s, they were almost extinct due to the demand for them in big-city restaurants. However, they survived and remain in the Smokies still today, albeit in far lesser numbers.

Mountain hunters usually utilized their dogs to flush grouse from the brush and killed them with a shotgun. The weapon's larger pellet pattern made it easier to hit the fleet birds than with a single rifle bullet. But Rich hunted grouse with a .22-caliber pistol. He killed the birds on the fly with a single shot to the head almost every time. Family members recollect Floyd leaving his home or hunting camp in the morning and routinely harvesting several grouse for breakfast—all killed with the pistol. Killing grouse with a single bullet from a .22 *rifle* would be an amazing feat, but using a *pistol* is even more astonishing.

The .22-caliber pistol and the .32-caliber muzzleloading rifle were the only two weapons that Floyd Rich ever hunted with. Floyd nicknamed the old rifle "Granny" because "the gun was as reliable as my old mountain grandma." Rich used the rifle to compete in almost every Cataloochee Beef Shoot ever held. He finished at or near the top of his age group from the time he was twenty-nine years old until the competition ended when he was in his late forties.

"Granny" was reliable on the hunting trail too. Rich killed more than one hundred bears and untold numbers of small game while using the old rifle. He sometimes used the .22 pistol to kill a bear at extremely close range when his dogs had a bruin bayed on the ground or if the animal was caught in a trap.

Floyd always kept two or three Plott dogs just for bear and boar hunting. Rich's early Plott canines were extremely ferocious and single minded when hunting bear. But grandsons Tony and Steven Rich maintain that the meanest dog their grandfather ever owned was a big redbone named Hitler. Floyd figured that a ferocious dog ought to be named after the world's most evil man. German tourists visiting nearby Maggie Valley were shocked when they learned the name of the dog and quickly vacated the premises after the hound snarled at them.

Once, while bear hunting deep in the Smokies, Floyd followed his Plott hounds into a small cove, up a steep slope and along a creek bank covered thickly in doghobble. It was nearly impossible to penetrate, and the bear finally eluded his dogs. But to his surprise, the cove opened up to a level plateau that housed the largest and oldest patch of ginseng Rich had ever seen. He described it as being similar to an enormous flowerbed. It was like finding a gold mine.

Rich fired signal shots for his hunting partners to locate him and led them back to the site. They immediately began digging and dug for the next two days and one full night. Floyd had to send others back to his cabin to bring washtubs to carry their bounty out. The ginseng berries were as big as tennis balls and the roots were thicker than a man's wrist. Some of the roots were so large that they had to be split before they could be dried and cured for the buyer.

Ginseng patches of this size are almost unheard of. But this was almost certainly the same field that Swain County legend Acquila "Quill" Rose stumbled across while bear hunting in the late 1800s. Rose decided to keep the location a secret, but when he later returned to dig it, he could not find it—and he never did. However, another Swain County sportsman, Sam Hunnicutt, claimed in his memoirs to have found the site. Hunnicutt stated that it was nearly two acres in size and located in a small, rugged hollow near Chimney Rock Branch in what is now the Great Smoky Mountains National Park.

Floyd Rich and his father Frank were masters of multiple skill sets—hunting, fishing, "sang" hunting, logging, trapping, target shooting, farming and liquor making—any of which would secure their place in mountain hunting folklore. By the time of his death in 1991, Floyd Rich's family had been hunting with distinction in the Great Smoky Mountains for more than a century. The Riches were firmly established as some of the best hunters in the region—but they had developed that reputation in relative obscurity.

However, the Fie Top Bear War would change that.

THE FIE TOP BEAR WAR

The story of the Fie Top Bear War is not included in any national or regional history books. The truth is, it wasn't an actual war—or least not in the truest sense of the word. There were no human casualties, no gun battles between opposing countries, armies or governments—and nobody really won. But for folks living in the Great Smoky Mountains from the late 1930s to the early 1950s, it was a real conflict with life and death consequences. A conflict—though on a smaller scale—not unlike the 1794 Whiskey Rebellion, when backwoodsmen balked at the federal government's attempts to regulate their liquor making. But in this case, it was Smoky Mountain hunters and farmers fighting to protect their livestock and homes from government-protected rogue bears. The war, along with the subsequent court battle, later achieved national attention due to a 1952 *Saturday Evening Post* article.

It was Frank and Floyd Rich, their relatives Preacher John Finger and Big Rufe Sutton and their neighbors Herbert "Hub" Plott and Glen Messer who were field marshals in the fight. They were led by Tom Alexander. Though greatly outnumbered by their opponents—marauding black bears and government officials—this mountain hunter militia wasted no time in striking back.

The seeds of the conflict were planted with the formation of the Great Smoky Mountains National Park (GSMNP) in 1934. Today, it is easy to appreciate the foresight that local, state and federal leaders possessed in creating the park. Without their leadership and determination, we could not still enjoy the largest wilderness area east of the Mississippi River. Moreover, had the park not been formed, greedy timber barons and real estate agents would have clear cut or developed the pristine wilderness to oblivion.

But this wasn't so easy for local mountaineers to understand when the GSMNP was first conceived. The formation of the park not only cost them their homes, but they also lost their communal hunting and grazing grounds. Former residents of the park, along with citizens of the surrounding area, considered hunting in the Smokies and allowing livestock to range there a God-given right.

It was even harder for them to grasp after the Tennessee Valley Authority completed Fontana Dam in 1944, submerging 68,292 acres of prime hunting land. Fontana Lake claimed the homes of 1,311 families and four thriving communities.

Ninety-nine-year-old Bryson City native Commodore Casada described the sentiments of most natives in a *Smoky Mountain Living* article published in 2009:

> *The business people were a little more educated and could see further out to where it would be an advantage. People like me, I just felt like there was something being taken away. You could go hunt, fish, camp out anywhere, anytime you wanted with no limit on anything you caught or killed. I had taken that as a right for me, and I saw it as being taken away after the park was established.*

Time has now healed those wounds for Casada. He readily acknowledges the values and merits of the GSMNP today. But it was difficult to do so back then, and it was made even more difficult by the government's reluctance to provide relocation assistance for the families forced out of the park.

As a result of this policy, most of the people thrown out of their homes relocated near the park boundaries to reestablish their farms. And it did not take long for the bear population to realize that the newly protected game lands provided them with a safe haven from hunters and trappers. Bruins would nightly raid nearby farms, killing cows, pigs and sheep, and then retreat to the refuge of the park to rest up for their next attack.

Hunters would track the bears back to their sanctuary only to be threatened with federal arrest warrants if they crossed the boundary lines to kill the rogue beasts. This only added insult to injury to the wounded pride of the displaced mountaineers. Threats of violence were exchanged with park officials and other law enforcement officers. Tensions ran high across the

Smoky Mountains, but by the late 1930s, they had escalated to a fever pitch on Fie Top Mountain and Hemphill Bald, in northwest Maggie Valley.

Little Rufe Sutton was only seven years old in 1940. But even today, at the age of seventy-six, he vividly recalls being scared to go out at night for fear of bear attacks. His uncle, Big Rufe Sutton, along with relatives Frank and Floyd Rich, were among the many elite hunters in the region who were routinely defending their homesteads from renegade bears. But it was one bear in particular—the legendary Honest John—that truly struck fear in all of them.

The massive Honest John—so named because he killed *only* to eat—was said to weigh close to eight hundred pounds. The beast had been terrorizing most of southwestern North Carolina and successfully evading the best hunters in the Smokies for more than a decade. Now that the GSMNP was formed, it proved to be even more difficult to subdue him. Frank and Floyd Rich, along with Big Rufe Sutton, were determined to change that.

Frank Rich had first encountered Honest John several years before when Frank's attempts to trap the bear resulted in John escaping minus three of his toes. For years, farmers and hunters identified the bruin by his large and distinctive two-toed rear paw print. Honest John left the area for a while after that, but in 1940, he had returned with a vengeance.

Frank Rich knew that the bear could not be trapped. It was simply too big. So he had obtained some additional Plott hounds from Von Plott to beef up his dog pack for a frontal assault on Honest John. After several more attacks and equally as many escapes, Frank, Floyd and Big Rufe Sutton struck Honest John's trail on Sheepback Mountain in northwestern Haywood County. The dogs finally bayed the bear in the Big Laurel section of the mountain near Maggot Springs Gap.

By the time the hunters reached the bear fight, several dogs had been killed or injured, but Frank Rich managed to shoot and kill the bruin. The size of the animal, combined with his unique rear paw print, left little doubt that it was indeed Honest John. Little Rufe Sutton told Steven Rich in 2009 that he clearly recalled the celebration that ensued when locals learned of Honest John's death. "It was a real big deal. REAL big. Sort of like a holiday. I remember it well. People came from all around to see the bear and get pictures of it. They made sure the foot was turned in the picture so you could see his paw."

Eighty-five-year-old Albert Rich, son of Jim Rich, concurs with Little Rufe on the story. A photo of Frank and Floyd Rich, Big Rufe Sutton, their dogs and several unidentified hunters beside the distinctive carcass further

The 1940 bear killed by Big Rufe Sutton, kneeling fourth from left, and Frank Rich, standing sixth from left. This bear is thought to have been "Honest John." *Courtesy of Steven and Linda Rich.*

verifies the tale. However, in fairness, there is no way to *absolutely* prove that this was Honest John. But it certainly *could* have been. There were no further sightings of the animal after that. Nevertheless, plenty of rogue bears continued to ravage the region. And the problem would only get worse.

Tom Alexander opened his Cataloochee Ranch resort on Fie Top Mountain in 1939. Though the ranch was a tourist attraction and later a ski resort, it was also a working farm. Alexander had hundreds of cattle and sheep grazing on the slopes of Fie Top and Hemphill Bald. He counted on them as a supplemental source of income as well as food for his tourist business. Most of Alexander's neighbors depended on cattle and sheep as a primary source of income and food for their families. They could ill afford to lose even one of their animals.

Yet by the summer of 1945, marauding black bears were leaving their government-protected dens to kill domestic livestock almost every night. To make matters worse, the bear population had soared to record levels during the ten years since the park was formed—and so too had the livestock killings. Protests to government officials were to no avail, and the situation continued to worsen.

Frank and Floyd Rich were called in to hunt the bears. But even these skilled nimrods and their famous Plott hounds were of no use, as they were forced to stop in hot pursuit at the park borders or risk arrest. Tom Alexander then recruited the Riches, along with Preacher John Finger, to trap the bears for him before they could escape back to the park.

But technically this was illegal too. North Carolina wildlife laws maintained that once a bear left its refuge on federal lands, it became a state-protected animal. As such, the bear could only be hunted or trapped during the officially designated hunting season from October to January. So even chasing the bears back into the park—or hunting or trapping them outside their sanctuary—was illegal out of season. Bruins living in the park basically had free reign to kill livestock and raid farms nine months out of the year. Legally, they could not be killed, hunted or trapped even *outside* the park, and they could *never*, under any circumstances, be killed *inside* their sanctuary.

This did not deter the Rich clan. After all, they had spent much of their lives avoiding federal prosecution and making liquor, so adherence to federal or state wildlife laws was not an issue for them. And it was even less of an issue when bears were depriving them and their employer of their livelihood. The Rich boys started setting their bear traps. The Fie Top Bear War had begun. The bears were winning—for now.

Many of the hardcore hunters in the mountains detested bear traps simply because of the danger they posed to innocent folks if not marked properly. Plus, it was difficult for even the heaviest steel trap to contain an injured and angry bear. But Floyd and Frank Rich were masters of this brutal art.

If the trap wasn't set just right, it often would snap up and flip over, catching the bear only by its toes. As in the case of Honest John, the bruin might lose a few claws or toes, but it could usually escape. The Riches avoided this by carefully studying the track and the stride length of their prey. As expert woodsmen, the Rich boys knew that a bear will seldom step on a loose stick. So they set their traps with a stick in front of it—just far enough away to match the animal's natural gait—to force it to step over the stick and squarely into the trap.

Most traps were attached to a short, heavy chain with a stout, three-pronged hook on the end. Even if the trap was securely attached to the bear, the animal could still run away dragging the hook and leaving a clear, distinct trail. Eventually, as the hook dug into the ground or became attached to a tree or laurel, the bear would tire and stop. Frank and Floyd would follow the trail and dispose of the injured bear quickly.

As bears became wary of the traps, the Riches had to become more sophisticated in their trapping techniques. They would go to the site of a livestock kill and build a three-sided log pen around the sheep or cow carcass.

Bear trap and hide, circa 1949. *Courtesy of Louise Plott.*

Just inside the pen entrance, hidden in the dirt with a stick properly placed in front of it, they laid the trap. It was anchored firmly to the pen. Once the bear was trapped, it was held in the pen until the trapper arrived to kill it.

The more experienced bruins eventually adapted to this technique too. They learned to avoid the trap entrance entirely and instead climbed over the rear or side walls for their dinner. Bears were said to have often carried dead cattle as heavy as three hundred pounds over the fence and back to safety in the park.

By 1947, the Riches and their Fie Top trapper militia had began to turn the tide in the conflict. The bruins were losing. But not for long. Once state wildlife officers in Raleigh, North Carolina, got wind of this, they sent Tom Alexander a final official warning to order his men to stop trapping and hunting bears out of season or else face a stiff jail sentence. Furthermore, they added that they planned to send the local game warden to confiscate their traps.

Alexander responded with a warning of his own. He would kill any man who tried to take his traps or those of his employees. With the government's bluff called, the Rich boys went right back to work hunting and trapping outlaw bears. The feuding groups were at an impasse as tensions continued to heighten.

Local game officials like Mark Hannah sympathized with their neighbors, but they were obligated to follow orders. Their bosses in Raleigh didn't want to be challenged by a bunch of (to them) renegade hillbillies. The trappers did not want to get arrested, but by the same token, they felt honor bound to protect their property. It was a serious dilemma.

News of the conflict quickly spread beyond the mountains. Newspapers across the nation covered the story. Feature writer Harold Martin came to Maggie Valley in the late 1940s to document the events. Martin later summarized part of the story in a 1952 *Saturday Evening Post* article entitled "Bears Are No Darn Good!"

State officials, not wanting any more adverse publicity, called a truce and asked to negotiate with the trappers. The two groups met in Waynesville, North Carolina, and argued for more than two hours before reaching a compromise—a compromise that still today rates as one of the worst and most inhumane decisions ever made by government wildlife officials.

The locals could continue to trap rogue bears at the site of a livestock kill. But they could *not* kill the bear. Instead, they were instructed to hogtie the wounded animal and then turn the bruin over to wildlife officials, who would take the bear and release it elsewhere.

Reluctantly, Alexander and the Riches agreed. Shortly after that, another bear was trapped and a game warden was summoned to aid in the capture. The official attempted to lasso the beast with a chain. The angry bear was having none of that. He jerked the chain from the officer and promptly sat down on it as he snarled at his opponents. After heated debate, the warden instructed the trappers to shoot and kill the animal.

The next incident was even worse. It took fifteen trappers to hogtie a trapped bear with heavy rope, but not before the enraged brute injured Tom Alexander. Finally, after three hours of grueling, dangerous work, the men managed to tie the animal to a stout pole and carried it toward the warden's truck, less than a mile away. After two more hours, they finally reached the vehicle, where the poor, distressed beast took a deep breath and died.

The state officials agreed that this method was not only impractical but it was also inhumane. So they allowed the trappers to quickly kill the bruin at the trap site, but with one condition: the men could *not* keep the meat or hide. They had to donate it to the state government, which then dispersed it to the poor.

Frank and Floyd Rich found this particularly insulting. The Rich clan wanted their game harvest to feed their own families. They preferred to distribute the meat amongst their hunting party in the traditional manner described in the chapter "Little George." They refused to comply with the law. Tom Alexander agreed, yet again defying game officials. The Fie Top Bear War had reached another standoff. But this time the government decided to just ignore the infractions of the militia and allowed them to continue their old-time ways. However, the war flared up again in the fall of 1948.

The mast crop was especially poor that year, yet the bear population was heavier than ever. This proved to be a deadly combination, as it again forced animals out of the park on nightly foraging raids. Tom Alexander had lost more than $10,000 worth of cattle to bear attacks. Though they had never really stopped, the Rich family and their friends began to set even more bear traps to combat the attacks. The government could no longer turn the other cheek. It again threatened the trappers with arrest. And again the trappers responded in kind with threats of violence to anyone who prevented them from protecting their farms.

As the Riches escalated their hunting and trapping of bears, Alexander further alienated the officials when he began billing them for his killed livestock, which they refused to compensate him for. Things reached a boiling point when a huge, old outlaw two-toed bear that had previously escaped

The Fie Top Bear War

Tom Alexander (left) and Glenn Messer with the cattle-killing bear that resulted in the 1952 arrest of Alexander. *Cataloochee Ranch Collection.*

them killed a seven-hundred-pound prize heifer owned by the Messer family. The marauder returned the following night to kill a six-hundred-pound steer owned by Alexander.

The beast had proven too big to trap. Alexander again called on the Rich and Messer families, as well as others, for assistance—this time to track and hunt the bear down with their dogs. A total of eighteen hunters and their Plott hounds soon located the bear and identified it by its unusual paw print as it ran toward the park. Like Honest John, this big bear was missing three toes. But unlike John, the missing toes were on its right forepaw. The rogue bruin crossed over the boundary, probably thinking that it was safe. But not this time, as the hunters entered the park and killed the beast about half a mile inside the sanctuary.

The men dragged the carcass back to Cataloochee Ranch, skinned the animal and divided the meat in the traditional manner. Alexander kept the unique two-toed front paw and froze it as proof to the authorities that the hunters had killed the right bear. He then notified the proper officials of what had happened and took full responsibility for the killing, refusing to implicate the Riches or his other hunting neighbors.

Within two days after the incident, the FBI and the Department of the Interior had been called in by federal park officials to investigate the matter. Soon after, Alexander was instructed by a U.S. marshal to turn himself in to face federal charges for killing a protected animal within the park, carrying a firearm in the park and conspiracy to molest a bear. Though he was not actually on the hunt, Alexander, by his own admission, had authorized it. And as the leader of the Fie Top hunters and trappers, federal authorities clearly planned to make an example of him. A court date was set for November 12, 1952, at the federal courthouse in Asheville, North Carolina.

Alexander drove to his trial accompanied by several of the hunters—Big Rufe Sutton, Haynes Messer, Glen Messer, Ralph Campbell and possibly Frank and Floyd Rich. Tom also brought the frozen two-toed bear paw packed in a box as evidence. The hunters planned to testify that Alexander was not on the hunt. Upon his arrival at the courthouse Alexander asked and received permission to store his frozen piece of evidence in a closet in the U.S. marshal's office.

Due to the nationwide notoriety of the Fie Top Bear War, the courtroom was full of spectators and news media. Tensions were high as Judge Wilson Warlick called the court to order. Alexander's attorney, Roy Francis, made the argument that his client was not in the park, did not take firearms or dogs into the park and did not kill the bear. As the trial progressed through the day, Francis called a steady stream of witnesses to the stand, all of whom verified that Alexander was not present on the hunt.

Francis further argued that Alexander and his neighbors had the legal rights to defend their property. He reasoned that if a citizen can protect his home from a human intruder or thief, why can't he protect his property from an animal?

The prosecution countered that the law that legally permits a man to shoot a thief in his home does not permit him to kill the robber the next time you see him. More significantly, they charged, if Alexander did not make the illegal bear kill he certainly authorized it. The district attorney then called a number of the hunters to the stand and asked them specifically who killed the bear. All of the mountaineers responded in kind—they were not exactly sure who killed the animal. After all, there were almost twenty hunters in the party and it was impossible to say for sure who had shot the beast. (Later reports indicate that it was Ralph Campbell.)

After repeated failed attempts to break the hunters, the district attorney called Big Rufe Sutton to the stand. The attorney pointedly asked Sutton who had killed the bear. Like his neighbors, Rufe feigned confusion as to who was guilty. Exasperated, the lawyer finally asked Sutton exactly where the bullet came from that killed the bear.

Big Rufe wryly replied, "Well, I reckon it came from a gun."

The courtroom erupted in laughter as Judge Warlick banged his gavel to restore order. Shortly afterward, both attorneys made their closing arguments and the jury retired to make its decision. Late that afternoon, the jury emerged with its verdict. In *Mountain Fever*, Alexander describes the outcome of his trial:

> *Since I had not actually been present at the bear kill, my lawyers didn't call me to the stand, but called instead the mountain men who had been there. All testified that I had not taken part in the hunt though none seemed to know just who had killed that bear. When the jury came in with a verdict of not guilty late that afternoon, there was a wild burst of applause from the spectators.*

The mountaineers had prevailed again. Not only was Alexander acquitted, but none of the actual hunting party was implicated either. The frozen bear paw was never required for evidence. It was soon forgotten about as Alexander celebrated his victory.

About two weeks later, the federal courthouse in Asheville had to be evacuated as workers searched for the source of an inexplicable overwhelming stench. It turned out to be the abandoned, but now thawed, rotten bear paw. Alexander was later accused of intentionally hiding it, which he vehemently denied.

There was no clear-cut victor in the Fie Top Bear War. No legislation or amendments were passed to legally allow locals to protect their livestock. But Alexander's acquittal at the very least proved to be a moral victory for the locals. The Park Service wanted no more adverse publicity, and they did formally agree to some concessions. Oliver Rathbone was hired as a horseback ranger to patrol the park boundary line. Rathbone had the authority to kill any renegade bears leaving or entering the park. Furthermore, rogue bears could be killed *anytime*, even *in* the park, as long as a ranger was present.

Off the record, some officials conceded the difficulty of ensuring the presence of a ranger for every bear kill. They informally agreed to look the other way as long as the hunter/farmers did not take advantage of their unofficial compromise. By 1954, the bear problem was basically under control and the Fie Top Bear War was over.

Frank and Floyd Rich, the Sutton and Messer clans, along with the other members of Alexander's Fie Top hunting militia, happily resumed the old-time lifestyle that they had enjoyed for years. Tom Alexander continued to run the finest resort in the Great Smoky Mountains until his death in 1972. Alexander's family perpetuates his legacy at the ranch today as it remains one of the premier tourist lodges in the United States. It is a resort that truly honors mountain people, places and traditions.

Descendants of Alexander's hunting militia—the Sutton, Rich, Campbell and Messer families—all remain in the region today. They continue the legacy of their ancestors as they celebrate more than 175 years of Great Smoky Mountain hunting.

As the Fie Top Bear War drew to an end, one of Floyd Rich's Graham County hunting buddies had been hunting for almost four decades in the Great Smoky Mountains. And he wasn't yet even fifty years old.

NOT NARY A ONE

Many great hunters reside and hunt in the mountains of Graham County, North Carolina. But of this group, only one of them—Dewey Sharp—could claim to have hunted with many of the early golden age legends as well as scores of local modern-day nimrods. A good argument can be made that Sharp ranked at or near the top of *both* groups.

Certainly, his longevity contributed to his fame. Many mountain clans—including Sharp's—have hunted in the Great Smoky Mountains for a century or more. But Dewey Sharp was one of the few, and perhaps the only, individual to have hunted in the region for nearly a century *himself*. Sharp hunted small game for ninety-three years, starting at the age of six in 1915. At the age of sixteen in 1925, he began his eighty-year career as a bear hunter.

Sharp hunted bear until he was ninety-six years old and he killed a bear weighing over four hundred pounds when he was eighty-nine years old. Even at that advanced age, he was still physically capable of hunting. But he was no longer able to maintain his own stringent hunting standards, nor did he feel it was fair to his Plott hunting dogs to do so. So, in 2006, he gave his guns and his dogs to his friend Gerald Phillips and retired from the sport.

Sharp's record-setting longevity was only a part of his success. His remarkable hunting skills and his incredible physical stamina also account for Dewey Sharp being among the best all-time Smoky Mountain hunters. And, while he was no doubt a humble fellow, Sharp did not hesitate to offer a brief but honest reply when asked if he had ever met a better hunter than himself: "Not nary a one," he quietly answered and then continued: "I am satisfied that I made more tracks in Graham County than any man who ever lived. There were those that could almost keep up with me, but none that could out run me or out walk me."

Graham County native Marshall McClung—who is a modern-day man hunting icon himself—was a close friend of Sharp's and introduced me to him. McClung has served as director or rescue team coordinator for the United States Forest Service and the Graham County Rescue Squad for more than thirty years. During that time, McClung has rescued or found more than forty people in these dense mountain forests. Many local residents argue that McClung is the best woodsman ever born in Graham County. McClung disagrees. He maintains that no one knew the remote wilderness area better than Dewey Sharp: "I am honored to even be compared to him. Dewey Sharp was the last of an amazing breed of old-time mountaineers. I can only hope to aspire to his level of greatness."

Sharp's career as a hunter spanned most of the twentieth century and part of the twenty-first. But his story begins in the early nineteenth century. Ham Sharp, Dewey's grandfather, was a native of Yancey County, North Carolina. In the late 1830s, looking for better hunting grounds, he moved his family to the Long Creek section of Graham County. They were some of the first white settlers in the area. Ham was killed while fighting for the Confederacy in the Civil War. Ham's son Mark Sharp continued the family hunting tradition. He later taught his skills to his son Dewey, who was born on Long Creek in 1909. At the time of his birth, Dewey Sharp's family had been hunting in the Great Smoky Mountains for almost seventy-five years.

When I first met Sharp in 2008, I was amazed by his youthful appearance and vitality. He was almost ninety-nine years old, but he could have easily passed for sixty-five. Dewey told me of a childhood filled with hard work and good times living and hunting in the mountains. He particularly enjoyed old-time music and dancing. Sharp quipped, "If I hear good string music, I just can't stand still."

McClung remembers seeing his friend break into a "jig" at the age of ninety-six as he entertained his fellow voters while they stood in line to vote at the local polls.

Sharp learned to play banjo as a boy and was soon recognized as one of the best banjo players in the county. His first banjo was an old Sears and Roebuck model that he rebuilt himself. Before he was sixteen years old, Sharp was a favorite musician at local corn shuckings, weddings and parties of all kinds. And he was already building his reputation as a hunter as well.

Not Nary a One

In 1930, the hard times of the Great Depression forced the twenty-one-year-old Sharp to look for other work to survive. In addition to hunting and farming, Dewey also worked for various logging companies to help support his family. The pay was bad in the logging camps and the conditions were worse. Loggers generally made no more than a dollar a day, if that. Much of their pay went back to the company store to pay for housing, clothing and supplies. Sharp said that many men worked an entire week, six days, from daylight to sundown, and ended up *owing* the company money.

A Smoky Mountain logging camp. *Courtesy of Great Smoky Mountains National Park Archives.*

Loss of life and limb were common. There were no benefits. If a man got hurt or killed, his family was thrown out of their company home and a new employee moved in. Sharp laughed sadly as he described the company housing:

> *They weren't really houses. The truth is that they were no more than wooden boxes with a door and maybe a cut out for a window—but no glass in it. They usually had a hole cut out for a pipe for a wood stove to heat the place,*

> but sometimes not. Several single men could bunk in one box, and married couples with children were allowed their own box. And, when I say they were boxes, that is exactly what I mean—they were just wooden crates. They were about big enough to fit two on a flatbed train car when they moved them, though sometimes they could stack them and put four on.

I interrupted Sharp and inquired as to what he meant by moving them. He replied:

> I mean just that, move them. We only stayed in one place long enough to clear cut it. As we cut all the timber out, they built more railroad tracks to the next big stand of trees and then they moved us there. The company used a crane to load the boxes on the flatbed cars, chained them down and moved them to the next stop. We felt lucky to have a roof over our heads—such as it was—and to have a job. I was more fortunate than most in that I could have lived at home, but they liked you to live in the camps so they could keep track of you and make sure you were at work on time. If you missed work, got hurt or killed, they threw your family out and moved someone else who was waiting for a job right in. And, believe me son, they was plenty of people waiting for jobs back then. It was bad, real bad.

A logging train with crane. *Courtesy of Great Smoky Mountains National Park Archives.*

Not Nary a One

Did it take long to move, I asked? Sharp grinned and responded:

> *We got one day off on Sunday, to rest, go to church, or hunt, or move the camp. They wasn't going to move us on a work day and miss cutting any logs. I usually hunted after church if I could. I didn't own nothing but my dogs and the clothes on my back. So, no, it didn't take long for me to move. I just pissed on the fire, called the dogs and moved on to the next place they wanted us to work.*

When asked if he ever logged any original growth timber, Sharp answered, "Oh yeah, biggest trees I ever seen. Lot of them was bigger than twenty-five foot around—especially the poplars. And we cut all of them with a crosscut saw and axe. Wasn't no chain saws back then. Talk about hard work—I get tired just thinking about it."

Sharp was working for a logging company in late 1934 when he had an experience that still haunted him in 2008. He was asleep in the bunkhouse when he was jolted out of bed on New Year's Eve night. The ground shook fiercely for what seemed like hours, but it was only minutes, followed by an avalanche of boulders thundering down the mountainsides. No one was hurt, but it was a night that he would never forget. Marshall McClung checked local and federal geological records and confirmed that a severe

A huge poplar tree stump cut by loggers. *Courtesy of Great Smoky Mountains National Park Archives.*

A Shay locomotive with a load of timber. *Courtesy of Great Smoky Mountains National Park Archives.*

Not Nary a One

earthquake did indeed take place on that exact date—yet further testament to Sharp's incredible memory.

The next day, Sharp climbed to the top of the mountain above the camp near Tatham's Gap, North Carolina. There he found a massive hole where the ridge had literally split in half. The top of the mountain was separated four hundred feet long, ten feet wide and more than fifty feet deep. Boulders broken perfectly in half littered each side of the chasm like puzzle pieces. Sharp later took McClung to visit the location. Both men believed that the gorge was the result of the 1934 earthquake.

Through good times and bad, Sharp always hunted. Dewey loved all types of hunting, as well as trout fishing, but bear hunting was his true passion. He hunted with some of the most famous old-time bear hunters that ever lived—men like "Uncle Sammy" Birchfield, Nathaniel "Blaine" Blevins, Floyd Rich, Forest, Horace and Vic Denton, along with numerous members of the celebrated Orr clan, including Jake, John, Dallas, Andy and "Little Will" Orr.

Sharp was especially impressed with Newt Hooper and Forest Denton, both of whom he said "were almost as good as me," as well as with Cotton McGuire and Floyd Rich, whom he remembered as being "a real good hunters."

Dewey hunted with Swain County sportsman Sam Hunnicutt and even saved his life once while hunting near Hazel Creek, North Carolina. It seems that the duo had lost their dogs near Sugar Fork Gap while arguing about directions and eventually ended up having to spend a long, frigid night on High Knob. Sharp said that Hunnicutt was nearly frostbitten as Dewey managed to get a fire started in the snow. He made Sam a bed of dead honeysuckle near the blaze, and throughout the night Sharp scavenged for more dry wood to feed the flames. According to Sharp, the next day Sam acknowledged that Dewey's directions were correct and credited him with saving his life. This was high praise coming from Sam Hunnicutt, who once described himself as being a perfect hunter and fisherman. They unfortunately never found their dogs.

Sharp stated that he also greatly respected Swain County native Mark Cathey. "Uncle Mark" Cathey was arguably the greatest Smoky Mountain sportsman that ever lived. Dewey remarked that he hunted often with Mark on Hooper's Bald and enjoyed his company. Sharp added that he later let Mark borrow a gun on a hunt near Hog Jaw Gap after Cathey's rifle was broken beyond repair.

Though he hunted with these and other local legends, and was witness to over one hundred bear kills, Sharp often preferred to hunt alone with only his dogs for company. The reason was that most hunters could not keep up with him. Once while hunting with the noted moonshiner Sammy Birchfield, Dewey ran off and left him as Sammy took a shortcut to the bear tree. Dewey still beat Birchfield to the bear and killed it before Sammy arrived. Birchfield was astonished by this and told Sharp that no one had previously ever beaten him to a treed bruin.

When Sharp was in his late eighties, a group of young hunters in their mid-twenties expressed concern about the "old man" being able to keep pace. Dewey not only beat them to their designated meeting place atop a nearby mountain, but he also sat patiently for an hour whittling with his pocket knife as he waited for the younger men to arrive.

However, it was not just his stamina and longevity that set him apart from other great hunters. Sharp seemed to possess a sort of magical, innate second sense when it came to hunting. He described it this way: "Wild game just seemed to come to me. Somehow I could always see an animal first, or

Dewey Sharp and friends loading a bear into a truck. *Courtesy of Dewey Sharp*.

just sense where it was before anyone else could. I don't know any other way to explain it. I reckon it was a sort of a gift."

Another thing that was different about Sharp was his ability to kill animals humanely and cleanly with only one shot. Though he was an excellent marksman, his philosophy of one shot, one kill, had more to do with his reluctance to take a bad shot than it had to do with his superb shooting skills. Sharp was emphatic that if he could not get close enough to a bear for a clean kill shot, he would not take it. Nor would he kill anything but a boar bear, preferably a big one.

As a result, Sharp "only" killed twenty-one bears himself in his long hunting career. Though he cared little for body count totals or mounted trophies, his kills were usually huge bruins. The biggest bear that he ever harvested weighed over 550 pounds. Sharp killed it near Fire Camp Branch when he was seventy-five years old. It took him and three friends more than four hours to carry the massive beast back to Dewey's truck.

Yet another secret to Sharp's hunting success were his Plott hounds. Dewey firmly maintained that there were no better hunting dogs than Plotts. He preferred female Plott dogs, as they seemed to mind him better. His favorite hound was named Dinah. She lived to be almost ten years old. Dinah literally ran herself to death while on a bear race from Bee Knob to Little Buffalo, a distance of more than ten miles. Sharp sensed that Dinah always understood exactly what he was saying, and he believed that there was a unique bond between them.

Sharp added that Dinah loved to kill rattlesnakes and that she was bitten four times while hunting for big rattlers. Dewey nursed the dog back to health each time with a natural snakebite antidote that he made from wild touch-me-not plants mixed with warm, sweet milk.

Sharp obtained his first Plott dogs from a Cherokee Indian who lived on the Qualla Boundary near Birdtown, North Carolina. He could not recall the exact year but suspected that it was about 1930. Over the next seventy-six years, Sharp got other Plott hounds from local hunters. But as good as these modern dogs were—and they were outstanding—Sharp said that they were still somewhat different from the earliest old-time Plotts. Sharp maintained that these early purebred Plotts were much more aggressive than later-day Plott hounds. He compared them to bulldogs in that they preferred to fight and even catch a bear whenever possible. Or, as he described it:

> *They were real bad to fight a bear to the death and they would not stop until either the bear or the dog was dead. A lot of times they'd try and latch on*

> to a bear like they did on a hog. But a bear was just too big and too strong for them. You had to follow a bear trail close and get to the dogs fast, or else you would lose one or two of them every time.

Dewey greatly admired these ferocious hunting dogs, but their casualty rates soared, and hunters and breeders were faced with the dilemma of somehow toning down the vicious nature of the old-time Plotts. According to Sharp, they resolved the issue by breeding the Plotts to some local mountain breeds such as the Blevins dogs.

Blaine Blevins was the family member most often associated with the Blevins dogs. However, like many hunting legends, the dust of time has covered many details regarding Blevins and his hounds. But no one can dispute their integral role in Plott breed history. It is generally acknowledged that the two most famous Plott hunting dogs of all time—Gola Ferguson's Boss and Tige—had at least one-fourth Blevins dog bloodlines in their lineage. So there is no doubt of the importance of the Blevins family and their dogs to Smoky Mountain hunting history, nor is there any doubt of Blaine Blevins's actual existence. Hack Smithdeal and Gola Ferguson both recalled Blevins and his dogs living in a remote section of Graham County, not far from the Tennessee state line. Ferguson once said that the Blevinses' hounds were "some of the purest Plott dogs that he had ever seen."

The "Blevins dog" term is somewhat of a misnomer. Many historians believe that Blaine Blevins originally obtained his dogs from Montraville Plott and line bred and inbred them closely to keep his bloodlines as pure as possible—just as Gola Ferguson described them. Other breed scholars claim that the Blevins dog was a separate breed made up of several bloodlines, including mountain curs and Plotts. Sharp maintained that what we were really talking about was a purebred Plott dog with a bit of cur or hound mixed in to tone its aggressiveness down some. Sharp concluded that the end result of this cross was a dog "that would fight a bear close, but wouldn't try to tear the hide off it, and eat it."

Many renowned Smoky Mountain hunters kept Plott dogs. But Sharp believed that Blaine Blevins, along with the Denton and Lovin clans, had the best Plott hounds. When asked what they looked like, Dewey described them this way:

> They were various shades of brindle, and the Blevins dogs in particular were almost solid black or coal colored, or else had a black saddleback. But I saw some that were a red buckskin color too, as well as some red brindle

dogs. To be such aggressive dogs, they had a pretty cold nose. They were keen trailers. They were just fine all-around dogs.

But why was information about Blaine Blevins so hard to find? Sharp responded that the answer was simple. Blevins preferred to keep a low profile to avoid revenuers. Nathaniel "Blaine" Blevins was well known for several things—his musical talent, his outstanding dogs and most of all for making superb liquor.

Like his contemporary Quill Rose, of neighboring Swain County, Blevins chose to live "off the grid." He resided in a rugged and remote section of Graham County right on the Tennessee border, near the head of Santeetlah Creek. This allowed Blevins a place to not only hunt in peace, but more importantly to make moonshine and avoid the law.

Sharp distinctly recalled playing music with Blevins at his isolated home in about 1925. Dewey was only sixteen when he met Blaine, and he remembers him as being about forty-five years old, maybe older, then. Sharp further described Blaine Blevins as being a big, strong and well-respected man who was greatly appreciated as a fiddler and guitarist. Blevins was reportedly also quick tempered and he did not mind settling an argument with his fists.

I asked Sharp to clarify Blevins's name—was it Nathaniel or Blaine or both? Dewey said that he did not know for sure if Blaine was a nickname or a middle name, or if it was an alias used to confuse the law. But Sharp had no doubts that it was the same fellow. He then shared a story about a memorable shindig at the Blevins homestead.

It was Christmastime and there was snow on the ground as a crowd gathered for a picking party at the Blevins cabin. It was so cold that Blaine allowed his dogs to come inside and lay by the hearth or lounge at the feet of his visitors. Tables and furniture had been pulled back to make room for dancing. Dewey Sharp, Doc Stewart and Blaine Blevins tuned their instruments in anticipation of a long night of musical fun. There was plenty of food and even more liquor available, as Blevins kept an open barrel of homebrew with a dipper in it for his guests. Sharp remembered it like this: "Anytime anyone would want a sup of liquor, why, they'd just take the dipper and get some. If they ran out, Blaine had plenty more."

Dewey recollected Doc Stewart as being about the same age as Blevins and that he had a big, bushy moustache. Stewart was acclaimed as one of the best fiddle players in the region. Doc and Blaine were best friends and hunting buddies, but they were known to argue a lot—especially when they were drinking.

Not Nary a One

Dewey Sharp at age eighty with a bear he killed. *Courtesy of Dewey Sharp.*

Sharp said that it was as fine a frolic as he had ever attended. The musicians played until sometime early in the predawn hours, when most everyone else had either gone home or bedded down there for the evening. Stewart suggested that the pickers call it a night, too, but Blevins insisted that they keep playing. An argument ensued between the two friends and nearly resulted in fisticuffs. But a compromise was reached when Stewart agreed instead to take a break, get something to eat and then continue playing.

There wasn't much food left, but Stewart managed to find some cold cornbread and pickled ramps to eat. He then washed it down with a dipper or two of moonshine. They shortly resumed their music, when Stewart suddenly stopped and violently vomited across the room. Dewey related that the stench was overwhelming: "I have been in the dirtiest hog pens that smelled a LOT better. It was the worst thing that I have ever smelled in my

Dewey Sharp and friends on a bear hunt. *Courtesy of Dewey Sharp.*

entire life. I quit playing and got out of there." It was so bad that even the famous Blevins dogs vacated the premises and ran outside to sleep in the frigid snow. Stewart had put a quick end to a classic party.

As Sharp concluded the Blevins saga, I asked him if he could take me to the location of the Blevins homestead. Dewey assured me that he could. We later made plans to visit the site in early August 2008. It was a trip that we would never make. Dewey Sharp died unexpectedly on August 5, 2008. He was two weeks short of celebrating his ninety-ninth birthday.

Dewey Sharp was a remarkable person but virtually unknown outside his native Graham County. Not only did his family hunt in the Smokies for more than 170 years, but Sharp hunted in these mountains for almost a century *himself*. Few, if any, hunters have ever made that claim—or ever will.

Almost two centuries of Sharp family hunting traditions died with Dewey Sharp. He left no heirs to carry on their sporting legacy. This is a scenario that is increasingly common in the Great Smoky Mountains and across the United States. It is a scenario that, if left unresolved, will likely result in dire consequences to both our heritage and our environment.

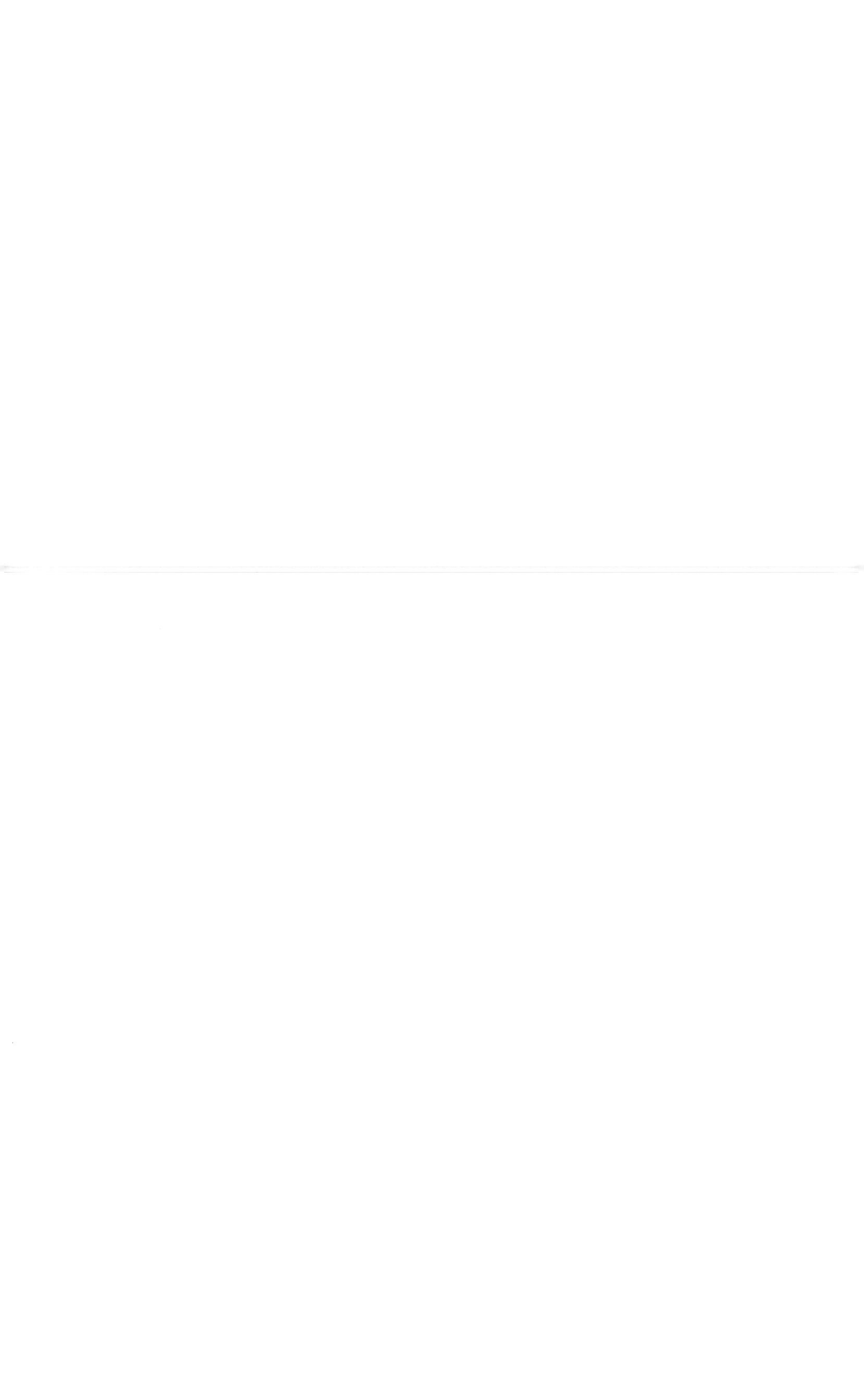

DUYUKTV-THE RIGHT WAY

Will hunting still play a prominent role in Smoky Mountain culture one hundred years from now? Will there still be mountain hunting clans continuing their legacy in the twenty-second century? It is hard to say for sure.

At the conclusion of my last book, I expressed optimism that as long as there are people in the Great Smoky Mountain region there will always be hunting. And I still believe that to be true. However, I am concerned that in one hundred years there will be only a few hunting families left who have hunted here for a century or more.

Traditional Cherokee culture is based on a simple sense of balance known as *Duyuktv*, or "the right way." The Cherokee basically believed that a careful balance had to be maintained in all aspects of their lives. Part of this balance pertained to hunting rituals—taking *only* what was needed, wasting nothing and utilizing all parts of the animal.

Duyuktv was disrupted in the Great Smoky Mountains from the mid-1700s to the mid-1900s. Entire species of animals and their habitat were eradicated for profit and pleasure by hunters, trappers and land barons. The end result was a cultural and environmental disaster.

With the development of new game, gun and environmental laws, game refuges and national parks, *Duyuktv* was slowly restored by the mid-1900s. Wildlife began to make an amazing return. It was a resurgence that once again gradually disrupted the balanced way of nature. Today, that comeback, combined with a decrease in hunters and a host of other serious environmental issues, indicates that there will be grim consequences for this latest disruption of *Duyuktv*. There is ample scientific evidence to support this conclusion.

The overall number of hunters in the United States has dropped 10 percent in the past decade. Small game and bird hunters declined by over 30 percent. In a 2008 *Sports Illustrated* article about the future of hunting, Matthew Teague surmised, "Outdoor activity is decreasing. Americans are becoming an indoor people. 21st century Americans talk about the environment, but they navigate websites not rivers."

In the same article, Nicholas Throckmorton of the U.S. Wildlife Service says, "What we are seeing among young people is nature deficit disorder."

Harvard biologist Daniel Lieberman adds, "We're shocked by things that should be natural and normal, like killing the animals that we eat. But we think nothing of buying meat on a Styrofoam tray wrapped in plastic."

The demise of hunting culture in the Smokies, and indeed the decline of the sport in general, is viewed as a good thing by many critics and so-called environmentalists. Yet Teague cautions these detractors: "What critics do not realize is that as hunters have stepped back, the animals (especially predators) have come forward—with potentially disastrous consequences for us all."

Valerius Geist, professor emeritus of environmental science at Calgary University, concurs with Teague and offers a scientific term for this natural imbalance: the recolonization by wildlife. Geist maintains that the first sign of this recolonization is the huge increase in herbivores. Statistics support his claim. *Sports Illustrated* reported that deer/car collisions increased 15 percent nationwide over the past five years, resulting in more than $1 billion in property damage and 150 human lives lost.

Professor Geist believes that we are just now entering the second phase of recolonization—an increase in carnivores and predators. He concludes that the third phase of the process will be "parasites and diseases (in animals and humans) returning in full force." Statistics appear to support these points as well. Bear populations, as well as their attacks on humans, have dramatically increased, and it is predicted that these attacks will increase in both numbers and ferocity.

Kim Delozier, bear expert for the GSMNP, believes that bears now see people as a food source: "We don't like to think about it—people come up with other reasons—but I believe these attacks are predatory." Joe Clark of the U.S. Geological Survey concludes that it is a simple case of more bears and humans forced to interact due to the growing populations of both species.

Duyuktv—The Right Way

University of Tennessee wildlife expert Mike Pelton told the *Knoxville Sentinel* newspaper in 2008: "There are more bears being harvested between Pennsylvania and Georgia than even existed in the 1970s. There is a concern by some state agencies that there aren't enough bears being harvested, that we are exceeding the point at which it is acceptable (safe) to have so many bears around."

The problem isn't just in the Great Smoky Mountains. New Jersey had fifty-two reports of home invasions by bears in 2007, and three hundred bears were killed by vehicles in Pennsylvania that same year. Cougar attacks on people are now common in the western United States. Perhaps most disturbing was the 2005 death of Canadian wildlife researcher, Kenton Carnegie. Carnegie, an unarmed vegetarian, was killed by a wolf as he went for an after dinner walk. It was the first documented wolf attack on humans in North American recorded history. This species was almost extinct a few decades ago but has rebounded in record numbers—and is now much more aggressive.

Just as Professor Geist predicted, animal-borne diseases are rising at a record pace. Rabies cases in North Carolina have increased 100 percent yearly since 1996. Lyme disease and Rocky Mountain spotted fever cases are also on the rise.

A combination of more animals, more people, less habitat and a drastic decrease in hunters results in one *big* problem. Call it what you will—animal recolonization or the disruption of a balanced natural life—we could be heading for disastrous results if *Duyuktv* is not restored.

But all is not lost. With 12.5 million hunters in the United States generating nearly $23 billion in annual revenue, we still have a chance to restore *Duyuktv*. One way to do this is by education. Hunting opponents must realize that legal, law-abiding hunters are truly environmentalists and conservationists. We are doing our part to maintain the proper balance of nature. However, we must find ways to not only maintain, but also to increase our family hunting traditions. And at least for now, there are still mountain families doing their part to do exactly that.

At the age of seventy-six, mountain hunting legend Taylor Crockett jogged almost an entire day following his dogs on a hunt in the rugged Deep Gap and Standing Indian Wilderness area near the North Carolina–Georgia border. Crockett had few peers as a hunter, and in 1982 he said that Andrew "Andy" Blankenship was the finest young hunter in the southern mountains. Blankenship of Hayesville, North Carolina, won the prestigious Methven Big Game Hunter Award in 1986. Today, Andy remains one of the best hunters in the Smoky Mountain region, and he has passed his skills on to his son Andrew Blankenship Jr. Andrew Jr. is now winning awards of his own and is poised to continue his family tradition of hunting in the Great Smokies.

John Jackson of Boone, North Carolina, the 2006 Methven winner, was a protégé of Taylor Crockett's. Jackson continues to honor Crockett's legacy by not only maintaining the Crockett Plott dog line but also by also mentoring young hunters such as Jason Pitts and Will Hicks. It is his hope that these two youngsters will someday pass that knowledge on to their family and friends.

Charles Brown's family roots run deep in the Smokies. His father's clan has hunted here since the Civil War. His mother's family—the Burlingames—moved to Hazel Creek to work for Ritter Lumber in the early 1900s. They were friends and hunted with such mountain legends as Granville Calhoun, Horace Kephart and Mark Cathey, as well as numerous members of the Cable family.

Brown missed his senior prom in high school because he was snowed in on a solo hunting expedition in the Citico Creek wilderness area of the Cherokee National Forest. He knew that it was a bad storm but did not realize the

Charles Stratton Brown and his four-year-old grandson, Brody Nash, in 2009. *Courtesy of Amye Nash.*

Duyuktv—The Right Way

severity of the situation until a rescue helicopter landed to evacuate him. Charlie thanked the would-be rescuers but chose to finish out his week-long hunting trip alone.

After serving in Vietnam, Brown had a family of his own. He taught his daughters outdoor skills. His oldest daughter, Amye, was particularly interested and later put his teachings to use when she joined the Marine Corps and served in Iraq. Today, Amye Nash is a police officer and has a child of her own, Brody. Charlie is today passing those lessons on to his four-year-old grandson.

Can *Duyuktv* be restored to the Great Smoky Mountains, and indeed the entire United States? Yes—but only if our family hunting traditions and educational programs continue to grow, and if part of that education includes a heightened awareness and participation in the improvement of a broad spectrum of environmental concerns, including global warming and pollution. As hunting environmentalists, we must not only educate our own families, but we must also expand our horizons to include *anyone* interested in the sport or conservation in general. We must somehow also convince hunting opponents that the demise of our sport is *not* a good thing.

Failure to accomplish these goals could result in cultural devastation as centuries of mountain traditions rapidly disappear. Worse yet, it will adversely impact our environment for generations to come. The choice is ours, and hopefully it is not too late.

BIBLIOGRAPHY

Alexander, Tom. *Mountain Fever.* Fairview, NC: Bright Mountain Books, 1995.

Allen, W.C. *The Annals of Haywood County, North Carolina.* Spartanburg, SC: Reprint Company Publishers, 1977.

Andrade, Allan. *S.S. Leopoldville Disaster December 24, 1944.* Orlando, FL: Fern Book Company, 1969.

Benzo, Stephen. "The Secret Nobody Tells." *Historical Records of the 66th Infantry Division Veterans Organization.* December 1969.

Coggins, Allen R. *Place Names of the Smokies.* Gatlinburg, TN: Great Smoky Mountains Natural History Association, 1999.

Davis, Marti. "Number of Attacks Grows With Bear Population." *Knoxville News Sentinel*, September 8, 2008.

Johnson, Becky. "Against All Odds." *Smoky Mountain Living* 9, no. 3 (2009).

Levy, George. *To Die In Chicago—Confederate Prisoners at Camp Douglas 1862–1865.* Gretna, LA: Pelican Publishing Inc., 1999.

Maloney, John. "The Hounds of Plott Valley." *True, The Man's Magazine*, November 1951.

Martin, Harold. "Bears Are No Darn Good." *Saturday Evening Post*, September 20, 1952.

Plott, Bob. *A History of Hunting in the Great Smoky Mountains.* Charleston, SC: The History Press, 2008.

———. *Strike and Stay—The Story of the Plott Hound*. Charleston, SC: The History Press, 2007.

Powell, William S. *The North Carolina Gazetteer: A Dictionary of Tar Heel Places.* Chapel Hill: University of North Carolina Press, 1968.

Teague, Matthew. "A Most Dangerous Game." *Sports Illustrated*, November 24, 2008.

ABOUT THE AUTHOR

Bob Plott is the great-great-great-grandson of Johannes (George) Plott, who first brought the Plott bear hounds to America about 1750, and a great-great-nephew of Henry Plott, who introduced the breed to the Great Smoky Mountains about 1800. He has spent most of his professional career working either as a manufacturing executive or martial arts instructor, though he is now employed in the racing industry.

Bob's first book, *Strike and Stay—The Story of the Plott Hound*, won the 2008 Willie Parker Peace Award for best North Carolina historical book. His second book, *A History of Hunting in the Great Smoky Mountains*, was named one of the top fifty regional books by the *Asheville Citizen Times* and has received outstanding nationwide reviews. Bob is a member of the American Plott Association, the National Plott Hound Association and the North Carolina Bear Hunters Association. He lives with his family and their Plott hounds outside of Statesville, North Carolina. Visit his website at www.bobplott.com.

Visit us at
www.historypress.net